Tasty Dump Dinner Meals To Make Busy Days Easier

Donnie .P Milne

Introduction

This book redefines home cooking with a collection of recipes that elevate convenience without compromising on flavor. This culinary treasure trove introduces a spectrum of dishes designed to simplify the cooking process while delivering an array of delectable tastes. Whether you're a busy parent, a professional with a hectic schedule, or someone who simply appreciates the ease of one-pot wonders, this cookbook has something for everyone.

The brilliance of this cookbook lies in its ability to turn mundane ingredients into culinary masterpieces. Each recipe is crafted to be effortlessly prepared, making it an ideal companion for individuals seeking delicious and time-saving solutions for family meals. The diverse range of options caters to various tastes, preferences, and dietary needs, ensuring that everyone can enjoy the pleasures of a homemade dinner without the stress of intricate cooking techniques.

One standout feature of this cookbook is its emphasis on diverse cooking methods. From skillet creations to slow-cooker marvels, each recipe introduces a unique approach to crafting meals that are both convenient and satisfying. The cookbook offers a refreshing departure from complex cooking processes, focusing instead on the joy of assembling ingredients, setting them to cook, and indulging in the delightful aromas that fill the kitchen.

The recipes presented in this cookbook showcase the versatility of dump dinners, proving that simplicity doesn't equate to dullness. Instead, these dishes burst with vibrant flavors, demonstrating that even the busiest individuals can enjoy homemade meals that are a far cry from bland convenience options. With options ranging from comforting casseroles to sheet pan wonders, the cookbook encourages experimentation in the kitchen while providing a reliable roadmap for those seeking reliable and delicious results.

What sets this cookbook apart is its commitment to ensuring that the joy of cooking is not overshadowed by the demands of a busy lifestyle. Each recipe is a testament to the notion that anyone can create mouthwatering meals without spending hours in the kitchen. It promotes a sense of culinary empowerment, allowing individuals to take control of their dinner plans and savor the satisfaction of serving a homemade feast.

In essence, this book is a celebration of simplicity and flavor. It transforms the act of cooking from a chore into a joyous experience, proving that even on the busiest days, a delicious homemade dinner is within reach. Whether you're a novice cook or a seasoned chef looking for quick and tasty solutions, this cookbook is a valuable addition to your kitchen, promising a world of culinary delights with minimal effort.

Contents

1 *Dinner? Dump It!* 1

2 *Dump It in a Pot* 18

    CHICKEN POSOLE 20

    CHICKEN, BROCCOLI, SHELLS, ANDCHEESE 22

    CHICKEN CORDON BLEU OVERTOAST 24

    CHICKEN ALFREDO RAVIOLI 26

    COUNTRY FRENCH CHICKEN 28

    MOROCCAN CHICKEN STEW 31

    MEXICAN QUINOA 33

    FAUX PHO 35

    TUSCAN BEAN AND CHICKEN SOUP 37

    ONE-POT FAJITA RICE WITH BEEF 40

    ONE-POT TOMATO-BASIL PASTA 43

    ITALIAN BEAN SOUP WITH DITALINI 45

    QUICK SUNDAY POT ROAST 47

    TACO SOUP 49

    BAKED BEANS AND SAUSAGE 52

3 *Dump It in a Skillet* 56

    CHICKEN ENCHILADA SKILLET 58

    SOUTHWEST CHICKEN SKILLET 61

    ITALIAN-STYLE CHICKEN ANDVEGETABLES 63

    JUST PEACHY BARBECUE CHICKEN 65

    ORANGE-CHICKEN SKILLET 67

    CHEESY SMOKED SAUSAGE ANDPASTA SKILLET 69

    POTATOES, SPINACH, ANDKIELBASA 71

    IRISH HASH SKILLET DINNER 73

    BEEF STIR-FRY 75

    SKILLET STROGANOFF 77

    SKILLET LASAGNA IN A FLASH 79

    CHILI AND CORNBREAD 81

SHRIMP FRIED RICE 83

MEATBALLS WITH HOISIN SAUCE 85

ZUCCHINI, BLACK BEANS, AND RICE 88

4 *Dump It in a Casserole* 92

CHICKEN DIVAN 94

BROCCOLI-CHICKEN CASSEROLE 96

CHICKEN POTPIE... 98

CHILI PIE 101

KING RANCH CASSEROLE 103

SPANISH RICE 106

CREOLE CHICKEN 108

FRENCH ONION MEATBALLS... 111

CHEESEBURGER PARADISE PIE 113

CHEESY HAM AND TATER TOTCASSEROLE 115

BACON, POTATO, AND CHEDDARFRITTATA 117

PIZZA CASSEROLE 119

CRAB AND SHRIMP DELIGHT 122

NO-BOIL MAC AND CHEESE 124

MEXICAN BAKED EGGS 126

5 *Dump It on a Sheet Pan* 130

PEPPERONI FRENCH BREAD PIZZA................................ 132

VEGETARIAN PIZZA 134

BARBECUE CHICKEN PIZZA 136

ROASTED ONIONS AND POTATOESWITH CHICKEN 138

NACHOS SUPREME 140

IRISH NACHOS 142

SHIPWRECKED FRENCH FRIES 144

OVEN FAJITAS 146

OVEN-BAKED PARMESAN TILAPIAAND ROASTED CAULIFLOWER 148

ROASTED MIXED VEGETABLES 150

6 *Dump It in a Slow Cooker* 154

SOUTHWEST CHICKEN 156

SWEET ORANGE-GINGER CHICKEN 158

HONEY-CHIPOTLE CHICKENSLIDERS 160

WHITE CHICKEN CHILI 163

HAWAIIAN CHICKEN 166

CLASSIC STEW 168

ITALIAN BEEF SANDWICHES 170

SLOW-COOKER PEPPER STEAK 172

DR. PEPPER PULLED PORK 174

SMOTHERED PORK CHOPS 176

7 *Dump It in a Bowl* 180

GREEK CHICKEN SALAD 182

CHICKEN AND STRAWBERRY SALAD 184

BARBECUE CHICKEN SALAD 186

FAJITA SALAD BOWLS 188

ASIAN CHICKEN SALAD 190

BURRITO BOWLS 192

CALYPSO BEEF SALAD 194

WHITE BEAN AND TUNA SALADPROVENÇAL 196

SOUTHWESTERN BLACK BEANSALAD 198

SEVEN-LAYER SALAD 200

1 *Dinner? Dump It!*

. . . .

DUMP DINNERS—the concept doesn't sound very appetizing, does it?

Well, don't be deceived, for if it's not already, it's about to become your favorite type of cooking. In today's overscheduled world, we crave, but lack time to cook, the comforting meals we grew up eating. It's usually a miracle just getting the family around the table at the same time! With *Dump Dinners*, you can make those delicious meals, have them on the table with very little fuss, and continue the dinnertime memory-making tradition.

A dump dinner takes just minutes to make because you literally "dump" the ingredients in a pan and then warm them. Start with a variety of precut, precooked, and packaged foods and end up with the kinds of comfort foods that have the kids licking their plates and asking for more. These recipes are not only quick but also less expensive than you might think—especially when you figure in the cost of your time.

There's a dump dinner for everyone—whether you prefer skillet, oven, or slow-cooker meals. And, if you're new to cooking, don't worry. These recipes are created with you in mind. There is no need for special equipment, special techniques, or special ingredients—and they're so good you probably won't need storage containers for leftovers, either!

Some dishes are good for making ahead and freezing. When this is an option, the instructions are included with the recipe. You can make several dinners in an hour or so in an afternoon and enjoy more time away from the kitchen during the week.

Most of the ingredients needed are probably in your pantry right now, which makes the hardest thing about these dump dinners choosing which one to make tonight!

Why We Love Dump Dinners

Dump dinners are seemingly more and more popular every day. Their no-fuss, no-prep features let you focus on the fun, creative parts of cooking with time to spare. Dump dinners are also versatile. You can use any cooking method—from oven to microwave to even campfire cooking! So, dump the stress of family meal time and have some fun.

Very little hands-on time is required to get these meals on the table. These recipes rarely take more than 5 to 10 minutes of preparation time, and you'll find that many come together in less than 5 minutes. Most recipes can save you additional time when you double the recipe and freeze half for another meal. Imagine just pulling a bag out of the freezer and dumping it into a pan to warm. You'll notice that there are instructions for freezing many of the recipes in this book. If you're going to eat the dish right away, follow the first set of instructions. If you're going to freeze the dish for later, follow the To Freeze instructions. Please note: all the ingredients are in order for the immediate preparation instructions, not the To Freeze instructions.

The recipes are even easy enough that a child old enough to read and follow directions can help put a meal on the table when you are running late or feeling under the weather. In fact, these recipes are fantastic for getting the whole family working together in the kitchen. Take a rainy Saturday afternoon and form a family assembly line to prep several dinners at once for the freezer. It's just that kind of quality time that builds lasting memories.

Dump Dinners will help you make the most of the time you have. No more rushing in the door after a long day at work to get some sort of meal on the table while helping with homework and baking two dozen cookies for the class party. Unburden yourself from that parental guilt you feel when sitting in a fast-food restaurant again and wondering how to adjust the budget one more time.

The recipes here are based on common ingredients with popular flavors. Almost everyone will love them—from kids to grandparents. Dump dinners are also perfect for potlucks and parties. Have you been wanting to prepare meals that are easy to make, save time, and are totally delicious? Then, welcome to love at first bite.

AVOCADO: NATURE'S PREPACKAGED WONDER

One fresh ingredient you might want to keep on hand is avocado. This mellow fruit provides one way to add texture, nutrition, and fresh flavor to your dump dinners without a lot of additional preparation. You only need to peel it and slice it.

If you find a great deal on avocados, peel them, brush with freshly squeezed lemon juice, wrap in plastic wrap, put them in a freezer-safe container, and freeze. They'll be ready to use anytime you need them.

Tips for using avocados in your recipes:

* Check for ripeness by gently squeezing in the palm of your hand. A ripe avocado will be firm, but still yield to gentle pressure.

* Avoid avocados that are too soft or discolored.

* To prepare: cut into the avocado lengthwise until your knife hits the seed. Rotate the avocado around the knife. Give the avocado a quarter turn and repeat. Separate the quarters, remove the seed, and pull off the peel.

* Sprinkle the surfaces with freshly squeezed lemon juice to keep from discoloring.

* Store ripe avocados in the refrigerator.

Using avocado to perk up your meals is as easy as topping your finished dish with ripe slices or cubes. The fruit adds a cooling touch to spicy dishes, especially those with Thai, Southwestern, or Mexican flavors, and a dose of healthy fat and nearly 20 vitamins and minerals to your meals.

Ten Tips for Making Great Dump Dinners

1. **Go easy on the salt.** The commercially prepared ingredients you'll be using often contain more salt than you would add yourself. You may not need to salt your dishes at all—taste first to be sure.

2. **Vacuum seal dinners you freeze.** It's a great way to save time and create budget-friendly meals similar to those in the freezer section of your grocery store. Just dump the ingredients together and toss in the freezer. When you are ready to cook, thaw and dump the contents in a slow cooker. If you don't have a vacuum sealer, use resealable freezer-safe bags or other food-safe freezer containers.

3. **Thaw frozen meals before adding to the slow cooker.** Simply remove the meal from the freezer the night before and place it in the refrigerator to thaw. By the next morning, it will be ready to go into the slow cooker for dinner that night.

4. **Save money by buying in bulk.** Prep your bulk-purchased items and store in small containers to use as needed in each recipe. For example, buy a large package of ground beef, cook it all, then divide into one-pound portions for freezing. Use a food processor to chop several onions at once and you'll have them handy all week long—or measure recipe-size portions into freezer-safe bags and freeze until needed.

5. **Label everything you freeze with the contents**

and the date. If you don't, it can be difficult to know what's in each package and which to use first.

6. **Read the entire recipe and assemble the ingredients before you start.** There's nothing worse than getting halfway through a recipe and discovering you're out of one of the main ingredients.

7. **Keep ingredients similar when substituting one for another.** Pork can be substituted for chicken or beef in most recipes, but chicken doesn't usually work well in beef dishes, for example.

8. **Don't overcook.** Since most of the recipes' ingredients are already cooked, you just need to warm them through. Follow a recipe's suggested cook times carefully.

9. **Make a meal plan.** Take the time for this step so you know what ingredients you'll need for the week. Choose the recipes for each meal and try to vary flavors from one day to the next. Having more control over your meals gives you control over your budget and time, as well.

10. **Plan leftovers.** Make double the amount of rice you need for tonight and use the rest in a dump recipe later in the week or use up leftovers in other dump recipes.

Recommended Ingredients

There are some ingredients you will want to keep on hand to simplify meal times. Buy them in large quantities when they are on sale or you have coupons, and replenish your supply when it gets low. These will form the foundation for your dump dinners.

There are new products introduced every day with the goal of making your mealtime chores easier and faster. Keep an eye out for these and don't be afraid to try them. Some may not work for you, but others are sure to become favorites.

The following are some food items to have on hand. As you discover favorite recipes, there will be more ingredients that you'll want to add to this list.

Stocking the Shelves, Refrigerator, and Freezer

CANNED AND BOTTLED ITEMS

* Beans: used in many dishes, they come in lots of varieties and add both fiber and quality protein while keeping the budget in check. Some beans need to be drained and rinsed before adding to a recipe while others do not. Follow the recipe's instructions.

* Broth: beef, chicken, and vegetable are necessary to make clear soups and to flavor pasta, rice, and other starches.

* Chili: comes in a variety of heat levels and with beans and without and works well over pasta or rice for a quick dish.

* Condensed soups: a variety like cream of celery, cream of chicken, and cream of mushroom creates creamy sauces.

* Condiments and sauces: ketchup, marinara, mayonnaise,

mustard, salad dressings, salsa, and teriyaki create layers of flavors.

* Garlic (minced or chopped and bottled): available in the produce section of most stores, easily adds that fresh garlic flavor.

* Gravies: work like soups to make quick, easy meals served over bread, pasta, and rice.

* Vegetables: canned varieties like potatoes and carrots save time because they are already cooked. Open, drain, and dump!

DAIRY

* Biscuits (canned): use to top potpies or as a base for many dishes.

* Shredded cheeses: easy to measure and add to recipes.

DELI

* Hard-boiled eggs: conveniently cooked, peeled, and ready to go are usually found in the deli.

* Rotisserie chicken and other precooked meats: sliced turkey can be turned into a hot open-faced sandwich just by adding bread and turkey gravy.

* Salads (prepared): potato salad and coleslaw are good sides or additions to some dishes. Coleslaw is classic on a

barbecued pork sandwich, for example.

FROZEN FOODS

* Pie crusts: Use for quiches or potpies. Add a can of stew to a frozen piecrust, put a second crust on top, bake for 30 minutes, and dinner is served.

* Rice (precooked): found in many grocery stores both with the rice and in the freezer section. To save some money, cook a batch of rice and freeze it in recipe-size bags. A rice cooker is great for preparing rice ahead of time.

* Vegetables: broccoli, cauliflower, corn, green beans, and peas can be added with no prep and will save you time.

MEAT

* Chopped barbecued beef, chicken, and pork: available in tubs in many grocery stores. Put together barbecue sliders in a couple of minutes or use it for filling tacos.

PANTRY ITEMS

* Biscuit mix: easily whip up pancakes or create those "impossible" pie recipes.

* Bouillon powder: boosts the flavor of broths, sauces, and soups.

* Bread crumbs and seasoned croutons: add crunch, flavor, and

texture.

* Couscous: a Middle Eastern staple that cooks in minutes. This tiny pasta is light, fluffy, and a great substitute for rice.

* Dried herbs and spices: quick and easy ingredients add more intense flavors.

* Pizza crusts: prebaked so all you need to do is add toppings and warm them.

PRODUCE

* Vegetables (prewashed and cut): add freshness to your meals without spending all your time washing, peeling, and chopping.

Recommended Supplies

There are some items that can make dump dinners even faster and easier to prepare. They are not expensive and are available in most variety stores and on the Internet. As you expand your recipe repertoire, you may discover others that help you make the most of your meal-time prep.

* **Canning jars.** One-quart canning jars are great to put salads in, but that isn't all. Use them to store smaller-serving dump dinners in the refrigerator and freezer.

* **Food processor.** This versatile kitchen tool helps you chop and grate ingredients in seconds.

* **Freezer-safe bags.** These are the easiest and least expensive storage containers. Buy them in a few different sizes.

* **Labels.** Big shipping labels can be attached to your freezer containers with information about the contents, the date, and even cooking instructions written in permanent marker.

* **Microwave.** This is almost essential when it comes to warming dinners you made ahead and froze. What takes 30 minutes in the oven will only take about 5 minutes in the microwave.

* **Permanent marker.** Use this to label your storage containers because the ink doesn't smear or rub off.

* **Plastic storage containers.** Food-grade plastic storage containers come in many sizes and keep your dump dinners fresh in the freezer.

* **Scale.** A food scale helps when making meals in bulk by ensuring that all containers have equal amounts of food.

* **Vacuum sealer.** This kitchen appliance allows you to seal ingredients and complete meals in such a way that they stay fresh longer in the refrigerator or freezer. If you are making dump dinners for the freezer, it is indispensable.

DUMP DINNER VERSUS TAKE-OUT

Is it really easier and quicker to make a dump dinner than to head for your favorite take-out spot?

* You'll never wonder again if the person putting your French fries in a bag washed his hands.

* Even if you call ahead and order your food to-go, there's still driving to pick it up, looking for parking while you get it, and then driving back home.

* Never again suffer the heartbreak of getting home with take-out and finding that your order was placed incorrectly.

* Saving money feels really good. Making dinner at home can save you significant cash.

* Making a delicious dinner that the whole family loves is a satisfying task. It just feels good to watch your family happily chow down on something you made.

* There's nothing like hearing your 10-year-old tell her best friend you are the best cook ever.

* According to a study conducted by the National Center on Addiction and Substance Abuse at Columbia University, teenagers who grow up eating family dinners together not only get better grades,

but also are less likely to engage in risky behaviors like drinking and taking drugs.

* If you are dependent on fast food then suddenly get snowed in, you are likely to be very hungry for a while—or at least become more interested in the dog treats in the cupboard.

2 *Dump It in a Pot*

. . . .

SOUPS AND OTHER ONE-POT MEALS make dinner super easy, especially when you literally dump everything in, cover, and walk away. These recipes are designed to be quick and easy and have minimal ingredient preparation so you have more time to do other things— like help with homework or do a few minutes of relaxing stretches. You'll find some old favorites alongside international flavors that might just become new favorites.

No special utensils are needed, but you will need a two- to four-quart pot with a lid. Use something heavy, if possible; enamel covered cast iron is perfect. These heavier pots heat more evenly and hold heat longer— making your job even easier. Other than that, a wooden spoon is nice to have because it doesn't conduct heat, but any large spoon will work just fine.

These recipes are real time-savers, but you can save even more time by assembling several meals at once and freezing them. You can usually put together two weeks' worth of dump meals in about 15 minutes. At dinnertime, you only have to dump the contents into a pot (remember, it's a good idea to thaw first) and warm according to the recipe's instructions. It's that easy!

CHICKEN POSOLE

Serves: 4 Prep time: 2 minutes Cook time: 10 minutes

You can use leftover cooked chicken or rotisserie chicken from the deli for this warming comfort food with lots of Southwest flavor. Posole is a dish that's a mix between a soup and a stew. Spoon into bowls and garnish with fresh cilantro, diced avocado, a squeeze of lime, and a handful of shredded cheese. Round out the meal with a crisp salad and some cornbread on the side. Make a quick dessert with frozen waffles topped with cherry pie filling and a scoop of white chocolate ice cream.

. . . .

1 (8-ounce) package frozen mixed onions and peppers

2 (4-ounce) cans diced green chiles

1 (14-ounce) can white hominy, drained

2 cups shredded cooked chicken

1½ cups chicken broth

2 teaspoons ground cumin

1 teaspoon garlic powder

1 teaspoon salt

½ teaspoon chipotle powder (optional)

½ cup chopped fresh cilantro, divided

½ cup diced avocado, divided

. . . .

1. In a large soup pot set over medium heat, combine the onions and peppers, green chiles, hominy, chicken, chicken broth, cumin, garlic powder, salt, and chipotle powder (if using).

2. Heat for 5 to 10 minutes, or until warmed through.

3. Serve topped with equal amounts of cilantro and avocado.

TO FREEZE

1. In a large, labeled freezer-safe bag, combine the onions and peppers, green chiles, hominy, chicken, cumin, garlic powder, salt, and chipotle powder (if using).

2. Seal the bag, flatten, and freeze flat.

3. The night before cooking, transfer the meal from the freezer to the refrigerator to thaw overnight.

4. The next day, add the contents of the bag and the chicken broth to a large soup pot.

5. Cook for about 5 minutes over medium heat, or until warmed through.

6. Serve topped with equal amounts of cilantro and avocado.

TIP: If it's one of those days when everyone will be eating at different times, this recipe can still work for you. Simply add the ingredients to a slow cooker and cook on low for 4 to 8 hours. It will be ready when you are.

CHICKEN, BROCCOLI, SHELLS, AND CHEESE

Serves: 4 Prep time: 2 minutes Cook time: 10 minutes

Chicken, broccoli, and pasta shells covered in a creamy cheese sauce make this dish a regular family favorite. You can bake it if you like a crispy top—just put the ingredients in a greased casserole, top with the Cheddar cheese, and bake at 375°F for 20 minutes, or until hot and bubbly. Serve with a kale Caesar salad kit from the produce section and a chocolate mug cake made in minutes in the microwave.

- 1 (40-ounce) family-size frozen macaroni and cheese shells dinner, thawed
- 2 cups frozen broccoli
- 2 cups diced cooked chicken
- 1 (10.75-ounce) can condensed cream of chicken soup or cream of broccoli soup
- ½ cup milk, plus additional as needed
- 1 cup shredded mild Cheddar cheese

1. In a large heavy pot set over medium heat, dump the macaroni and cheese, broccoli, chicken, cream of chicken soup, milk, and Cheddar cheese. Stir gently to combine.

2. Cook for 5 to 10 minutes, or until the dish is warmed through, stirring every few minutes to keep it from sticking.

3. Add more milk if the mixture seems too dry.

TIP: Any family-size frozen macaroni and cheese dinner will work if you can't find shells. Other soups can be substituted as well—if you like a very cheesy sauce, substitute Cheddar cheese soup for the cream of chicken. For something different, add 2 cups of diced ham or cooked ground beef in place of the chicken.

CHICKEN CORDON BLEU OVER TOAST

Serves: 4 Prep time: 2 minutes Cook time: 5 minutes

Chicken Cordon Bleu is a delicious dish that's usually way too fancy for a weeknight meal. For many, it's out of the question for a weekend meal, too! You can get the entire flavor in this easy variation, though. Creamy Swiss cheese, salty ham, and tender chicken are the prominent ingredients in this blue-ribbon dish. A salad or some green beans make this a complete meal. A bakery apple pie is a delicious finish.

1 cup shredded Swiss cheese

½ cup shredded Monterey Jack

1 (10.75-ounce) can condensed cream of chicken soup

2 cups diced cooked chicken

1 cup diced ham

½ cup milk

4 slices toast or English muffin halves

1. In a large pot set over medium heat, combine the Swiss cheese, Monterey Jack, cream of chicken soup, chicken, ham, and milk.

2. Cook for about 5 minutes, stirring gently, or until the cheese is melted and smooth and the dish is thoroughly heated.

3. Spoon equal amounts over each slice of toast and serve hot.

1. In a large, labeled freezer-safe bag, combine the cream of chicken soup, chicken, ham, and milk.

2. In a small freezer-safe bag, add the Swiss cheese and Monterey Jack. Seal the bag and slip it inside the large bag with the other ingredients.

3. Seal the bag, flatten, and freeze flat.

4. The night before cooking, transfer the meal from the freezer to the refrigerator to thaw overnight.

5. The next day, remove the cheese packet.

6. In a large pot set over medium heat, combine the Swiss cheese and Monterey Jack with contents of the larger bag.

7. Cook for about 5 minutes, stirring gently, or until the cheese is melted and smooth and the dish is thoroughly heated.

8. Spoon equal amounts over each toast slice and serve hot.

TIP: Serve this over rice, biscuits, mashed potatoes, or noodles just as deliciously as toast. It is especially good spooned over thick-cut Texas Toast. If you like more crunch, add a sprinkle of crispy Panko bread crumbs just before serving.

CHICKEN ALFREDO RAVIOLI

Serves: 4 Prep time: 5 minutes Cook time: 5 minutes

Tender chicken, rich Alfredo sauce, earthy mushrooms, and delicate cheese ravioli are simmered together for a few minutes until the flavors blend and the ingredients are hot. Serve with a crisp salad, garlic bread, and a simple plate of grapes for dessert. This recipe does not freeze well as the ravioli can get gummy.

1 (12-ounce) jar Alfredo sauce

½ cup chicken broth

2 cups diced cooked chicken

9 ounces fresh cheese ravioli or chicken ravioli from the refrigerated section

1 (4-ounce) can sliced mushrooms, drained

1. In a large stockpot set over medium heat, whisk together the Alfredo sauce and chicken broth until smooth. Bring to a simmer.

2. Add the chicken, ravioli, and mushrooms. Stir to combine.

3. Simmer, uncovered, for about 5 minutes, or until the sauce thickens and the ravioli is tender.

TIP: Add some color and extra nutrition to this dish with fresh baby spinach leaves. There's no need to cook them ahead of time, just add to the pot during the last 3 minutes of cooking.

COUNTRY FRENCH CHICKEN

Serves: 6 Prep time: 2 minutes Cook time: 30 minutes

This "roast" chicken dish seems like it takes a lot of time and effort, but it is almost as easy as takeout. Serve with a crisp romaine lettuce salad, mashed potatoes from the deli or freezer section, a warm baguette, and apple waffles for dessert. Cook frozen waffles, add a scoop of ice cream, and top with warm apple pie filling and caramel syrup.

- -

1 (4-pound) whole cooked rotisserie chicken

¼ cup (½ stick) unsalted butter, divided into tablespoons

1 teaspoon bottled minced garlic

2 teaspoons dried Herbes de Provence

½ lemon, sliced

¼ cup chopped onion

1 (4-ounce) can sliced mushrooms, drained

¼ cup white wine

½ cup chicken broth

1 tablespoon truffle oil (optional)

- -

1. Place a large, heavy pot with a lid over medium heat. Dump in the chicken (breast-side up), butter, garlic, Herbes de Provence, lemon slices, onion, mushrooms, white wine, and chicken broth.

2. Bring to a simmer and cover. Cook for 20 to 30 minutes, or until heated through.

   Add the truffle oil (if using).

3.

4. Transfer the chicken and vegetables to a serving platter.

5. Carve and enjoy.

TO FREEZE

1. In a large, labeled food-safe freezer bag, combine the chicken (breast-side up), butter, garlic, Herbes de Provence, lemon slices, onion, mushrooms, white wine, and chicken broth.

2. Seal the bag and freeze.

3. The night before cooking, transfer the meal from the freezer to the refrigerator to thaw overnight.

4. The next day, place a large, heavy pot with a lid over medium heat. Dump in the contents of the bag.

5. Bring to a simmer and cover. Cook for 20 to 30 minutes, or until heated through.

6. Add the truffle oil (if using).

7. Transfer the chicken and vegetables to a serving platter.

8. Carve and enjoy.

TIP: This makes a light, delicious soup if you use about 2 cups of cooked, shredded chicken breast and 2 cups of chicken broth instead of a whole chicken.

MOROCCAN CHICKEN STEW

Serves: 8 Prep time: 5 minutes Cook time: 10 minutes

This chicken stew is exotic and comforting all at the same time. Serve in bowls over a mound of fluffy rice or couscous. You won't need much else—perhaps some bread to soak up the delicious broth. For larger meals, add a salad and finish with éclairs from the bakery or freezer section. Dust some confectioners' sugar over the éclairs to give them a restaurant-quality finish.

- -

2 tablespoons olive oil

2 pounds shredded cooked chicken

1 pound frozen baby artichoke hearts

1 (14.5-ounce) can sliced carrots, drained

1 cup chopped onion

4 cups chicken broth

¼ cup bottled minced garlic

1 tablespoon ground coriander

1 tablespoon ground cumin

1 tablespoon smoked paprika

1 teaspoon turmeric

½ teaspoon cinnamon

2 lemon slices

- -

1. In a large, heavy pot set over medium heat, dump in the olive oil, chicken, artichoke hearts, carrots, onion, chicken broth, garlic,

coriander, cumin, paprika, turmeric, cinnamon, and lemon slices.

2. Bring to a simmer and cover. Cook for about 10 minutes, or until heated through.

3. Serve over rice or couscous.

TO FREEZE

1. To a large, labeled freezer-safe bag, add the olive oil, chicken, artichoke hearts, carrots, onion, chicken broth, garlic, coriander, cumin, paprika, turmeric, cinnamon, and lemon slices.

2. Seal the bag, flatten, and freeze flat.

3. The night before cooking, transfer the meal from the freezer to the refrigerator to thaw overnight.

4. The next day, place a large, heavy pot with a lid over medium heat. Dump in the contents of the bag.

5. Bring to a simmer and cover. Cook for about 10 minutes, or until heated through.

6. Serve over rice or couscous.

TIP: The lemon adds brightness, but you can change it up with orange slices instead. They add a similar zing and a unique sweetness. It's delicious! Leftovers can be frozen for up to three months.

MEXICAN QUINOA
VEGAN, GLUTEN-FREE

Serves: 4 *Prep time:* 2 minutes *Cook time:* 15 minutes

Quinoa is a gluten-free grain featured in this quick vegan dump dinner. This is a handy recipe to have whether you just need a quick, meatless meal or are living a plant-based lifestyle. You won't miss the meat at all in this fiery dish. The squash adds an unexpected sweetness. If you can't find it, use cubed sweet potatoes. Your favorite salad and a dessert of fresh in-season fruit are all you need to make the meal complete.

1 (15-ounce) can black beans, drained and rinsed

1 (14.5-ounce) can diced fire-roasted tomatoes, undrained

1 (14.5 ounce) can corn, drained

1 (4-ounce) can chopped green chiles

1 (8-ounce) package frozen diced butternut squash

1 cup instant quinoa

1 cup vegetable broth

1 tablespoon bottled minced garlic

1 teaspoon chili powder

½ teaspoon cumin

¼ cup chopped fresh cilantro, divided

½ cup diced avocado, divided

1. In a large pot set over high heat, dump the black beans, tomatoes and their liquid, corn, green chiles, squash, quinoa,

vegetable broth, garlic, chili powder, and cumin. Stir gently to combine.

2. Heat until the mixture comes to a boil. Reduce the heat to low. Cover.

3. Cook for 15 minutes, or until the broth is absorbed and the quinoa is tender.

4. Top each bowl with cilantro and avocado before serving.

> **TIP:** If you're not vegetarian, one-half pound of cooked, shelled, and deveined shrimp or grilled chicken is a delicious addition to this dish. Add it about 5 minutes before the dish is done so it has time to warm, but doesn't overcook. Serve with a lime wedge for squeezing over the top before serving. It adds a bright flavor.

FAUX PHO

Serves: 4 Prep time: 2 minutes Cook time: 5 minutes

Pho is a meaty Vietnamese soup that is a little spicy. There are so many ways to make pho! Ramen noodles come in a variety of flavors, so try a few to discover which you like best. Serve with egg rolls from the grocery store and a dish of fortune cookies for dessert.

1 cup chopped cooked chicken breast

1 (4-ounce) can sliced jalapeños

1 (32-ounce) container chicken broth

2 cups organic baby spinach salad

1 tablespoon bottled minced garlic

1 teaspoon ground ginger or 1 tablespoon freshly minced ginger

1 tablespoon sliced scallions

2 packets Oriental-flavor ramen noodles

Chili oil, for seasoning (optional)

Lime slices, for seasoning (optional)

1. In a large pot set over medium heat, stir together the chicken, jalapeños, chicken broth, spinach, garlic, ginger, and scallions.

2. Remove the flavor envelopes from the ramen noodle packages. Set the noodles aside. Stir the contents of the flavor packets into the soup.

3. Bring to a boil and immediately reduce the heat to low.

4. Add the noodles to the pot and cover.

5. Remove the pot from the heat and let stand for 3 minutes. Separate the noodles with a fork.

6. Ladle the soup into 4 bowls. Serve topped with a drizzle of chili oil and a lime slice to squeeze over the soup (if using).

TIP: You can substitute leftover roast beef and beef broth for the chicken and chicken broth used in this recipe. It's delicious with a few slices of canned mushrooms added.

TUSCAN BEAN AND CHICKEN SOUP

Serves: 4 Prep time: 2 minutes Cook time: 10 minutes

This garlicky chicken broth is full of hearty, good-for-you ingredients. If you like lots of garlic flavor, use garlic bread slices on top instead of the plain baguette. You can also cook this in a slow cooker on low for 6 to 8 hours. This has so many good-for-you veggies you really don't need anything else but a crisp salad with plenty of croutons to round out the meal. Serve almond biscotti and coffee for dessert.

1 (8-ounce) bag frozen chopped onions

1 (14.5-ounce) can sliced carrots, drained

1 (14.5-ounce) can sliced white potatoes, drained

1 (15-ounce) can white cannellini beans, drained and rinsed

2 cups cooked chicken

1 (32-ounce) container chicken broth

1 cup organic baby kale salad

1 tablespoon bottled minced garlic

4 baguette slices, preferably a little stale

¼ cup shredded Parmesan cheese, divided

1. In a large pot set over medium heat, combine the onions, carrots, potatoes, cannellini beans, chicken, chicken broth, kale, and garlic.

2. Bring to a simmer. Cook for 5 to 10 minutes, or until the ingredients are heated through.

3. Ladle the soup into 4 bowls and float 1 baguette slice atop each.

4. Sprinkle each with 1 tablespoon of Parmesan cheese and serve.

TO FREEZE

1. To a large, labeled freezer-safe bag, add the onions, carrots, potatoes, cannellini beans, chicken, kale, and garlic.

2. In a small freezer-safe bag, add the Parmesan cheese. Seal the bag and slip into the large bag with the other ingredients.

3. Seal the bag, flatten, and freeze flat.

4. The night before cooking, transfer the meal from the freezer to the refrigerator to thaw overnight.

5. The next day, remove the Parmesan cheese packet. Set aside.

6. To a large pot set over medium heat, add the contents of the large bag and the chicken broth.

7. Bring to a simmer. Cook for 5 to 10 minutes, or until heated through.

8. Ladle the soup into 4 bowls and float 1 baguette slice atop each.

9. Sprinkle each with 1 tablespoon of Parmesan cheese and serve.

TIP: Substitute sliced kielbasa for the chicken for a delicious variation. If you need a vegetarian version, substitute vegetable broth for the chicken broth, add an extra can of beans, and omit the chicken.

ONE-POT FAJITA RICE WITH BEEF

Serves: 4 Prep time: 2 minutes Cook time: 10 minutes

When you crave Mexican food, there's nothing easier than these Fajita Rice with Beef bowls! Starting with precooked, preseasoned rice and fajita beef means it's only a matter of warming the ingredients. Serve with warm flour tortillas, a crispy side salad, and a margarita for great south-of-the-border flavor. Warm slice-and-bake chocolate chip cookies make it extra special.

....

2 (8.5-ounce) pouches Ready Rice with pinto beans or 2 cups cooked rice

½ cup beef broth

1 (8-ounce) package frozen mixed onions and peppers

1 (10-ounce) can tomatoes with green chiles

1 (15-ounce) can black beans, drained and rinsed

1 (1.12-ounce) packet fajita seasoning

1 pound cooked beef fajita strips

2 cups shredded Mexican-blend cheese, divided

1 cup prepared guacamole, divided

¼ cup sour cream, divided

....

1. Squeeze the rice pouches to break up the rice.

2. In a large pot set over medium heat, combine the contents of the rice pouches, beef broth, onions and peppers, tomatoes with green chiles, black beans, fajita seasoning, and beef strips.

3. Cook for 5 to 10 minutes, stirring occasionally, or until the mixture is completely warmed through.

4. Top each serving with ½ cup of Mexican-blend cheese, ¼ cup of guacamole, and 1 tablespoon of sour cream.

TO FREEZE

1. In a large, labeled freezer-safe bag, add the contents of the rice pouches, the beef broth, onions and peppers, tomatoes with green chiles, black beans, fajita seasoning, and beef strips.

2. In a small freezer-safe bag, add the Mexican-blend cheese. Seal the bag and slip into the large bag with the other ingredients.

3. Seal the bag, flatten, and freeze flat.

4. The night before cooking, transfer the meal from the freezer to the refrigerator to thaw overnight.

5. The next day, remove the cheese packet from the bag. Set aside.

6. To a large pot set over medium heat, add the contents of the large bag.

7. Cook for about 5 minutes, stirring occasionally, or until the mixture is completely warmed through.

8. Top each serving with ½ cup of cheese, ¼ cup of guacamole, and 1 tablespoon of sour cream.

TIP: You can make this with cooked chicken, pork, shrimp, or any combination you like. If you want it spicier, add some sliced jalapeños to each bowl before serving. Tired of rice? This is a good dish to try with couscous!

ONE-POT TOMATO-BASIL PASTA
VEGETARIAN

Serves: 4 Prep time: 2 minutes Cook time: 15 minutes

This easy Italian meal just needs a crisp salad and a couple of slices of garlic bread to complete it. The angel hair pasta cooks quickly and absorbs the flavors of the liquid it's cooked in to make this super-easy meal super-delicious, too. Change it up by using a whole-wheat pasta, if you like, but plan on increasing the cooking time. Sweeten things with ginger ale floats—scoops of lemon sherbet in a glass with ginger ale.

12 ounces fettucine pasta

1 (15-ounce) can Italian-style diced tomatoes, undrained

1 (8-ounce) bag frozen mixed onions and peppers

1 tablespoon bottled minced garlic

2 teaspoons dried oregano

1 teaspoon dried basil

½ teaspoon chipotle powder

2½ cups vegetable juice cocktail

2 cups vegetable broth

Salt

Freshly ground black pepper

¼ cup Parmesan cheese, divided

1. In a large pot set over high heat, combine the pasta, tomatoes and their liquid, onions and peppers, garlic, oregano, basil, and chipotle powder.

2. Stir in the vegetable juice and vegetable broth. Bring to a boil. Stir gently and cover the pot. Reduce the heat to low.

3. Cook for 10 minutes, stirring occasionally, or until most of the liquid is gone.

4. Season with the salt and pepper.

5. Top each serving with 1 tablespoon of Parmesan cheese.

TIP: If you're not vegetarian, you can add eight cooked meatballs, frozen or thawed, with the broth if you want a protein with this dish. If they are frozen, cook the dish a little longer and add a little more liquid to keep it from scorching.

ITALIAN BEAN SOUP WITH DITALINI
VEGETARIAN

Serves: 4 Prep time: 2 minutes Cook time: 15 minutes

An easy, budget-conscious dinner for a blustery day, this Italian Bean Soup with Ditalini is classic Italian comfort food. A garlicky vegetable broth is filled with pasta and vegetables. Change this up with fresh tortellini, usually available in the deli section of your grocery store. Simmer it in the soup for the amount of time directed on the package. The leftovers, if there are any, are even better the next day. Serve with a classic Caesar salad straight from the produce section and lemon pound cake with warmed blueberry pie filling spooned over it for dessert.

1 (32-ounce) container vegetable broth

1 tablespoon bottled minced garlic

8 ounces ditalini pasta

1 cup chopped onion

1 cup chopped celery

1 (14.5-ounce) can sliced carrots, drained

1 (14.5-ounce) can flat Italian green beans, drained

1 (15-ounce) can Italian-style diced tomatoes, undrained

1 (15-ounce) can white cannellini beans, drained and rinsed

1 teaspoon dried oregano

1 cup grated Parmesan cheese, divided

4 baguette slices, toasted

1. In a large soup pot set over medium-high heat, combine the vegetable broth and garlic. Bring to a boil.

2. Stir in the ditalini. Cook for 10 minutes, or until the pasta is tender. Reduce the heat to low.

3. Stir in the onion, celery, carrots, green beans, tomatoes and their liquid, cannellini beans, and oregano. Simmer for about 5 minutes more, or until warmed through.

4. Stir in ½ cup of Parmesan cheese.

5. Ladle the soup into 4 bowls. Float 1 baguette slice on top of each.

6. Top each bowl with 2 tablespoons of the remaining Parmesan and serve.

TIP: Most large grocery stores have prepared raw vegetables in the produce section. You can often find chopped onions, chopped celery, and other commonly used vegetables. These products can save you time and probably won't cost much more than the regular versions.

QUICK SUNDAY POT ROAST

Serves: 4 Prep time: 5 minutes Cook time: 10 minutes

Can you imagine a slow-cooked pot roast dinner in just 10 minutes? Start with a prepared pot roast, add a few ingredients of your own, and just warm it up. While the roast is warming, you'll have just enough time to slip some brown-and-serve rolls into the oven and a bakery chocolate cake on the table. Grandma would be proud.

1 (15-ounce) fully cooked pot roast in gravy, usually found in the meat or freezer aisle

2 (14.5-ounce) cans sliced carrots, drained

2 (14.5-ounce) cans whole potatoes, drained

1 (4-ounce) can mushroom caps or slices, drained

½ cup red wine or beef broth

Salt

Freshly ground black pepper

1. Into a large, heavy pot set over medium heat, dump the pot roast and gravy, carrots, potatoes, mushrooms, and red wine. Season with salt and pepper.

2. Bring to a simmer and cover. Cook for about 10 minutes, or until the roast's interior is heated through.

3. Serve.

TO FREEZE

1. In a large, labeled freezer-safe bag, combine the pot roast and gravy, carrots, potatoes, and mushrooms. Season with salt and pepper.

2. Seal the bag and freeze.

3. The night before cooking, transfer the meal from the freezer to the refrigerator to thaw overnight.

4. The next day, place a large, heavy pot over medium heat. Dump in the contents of the bag.

5. Add the red wine.

6. Bring to a simmer and cover. Cook for about 10 minutes, or until the roast's interior is heated through.

7. Serve.

TIP: Instead of red wine or beef broth, use ¼ cup of condensed French onion soup and ¼ cup of water. It adds a deeper flavor to the gravy. Be mindful of how much salt you add as the onion soup is salty on its own.

TACO SOUP

Serves: 4 Prep time: 5 minutes Cook time: 10 minutes

Nearly everyone likes tacos, and this dish has all of that taco flavor plus the cold-weather comfort of a bowl of soup. Serve with a wedge of lime—squeezing the lime over the hot broth just before eating it enhances and brightens the flavors. A bowl of corn chips are a crunchy complement. A chipotle and Cheddar salad kit from the produce section makes a delicious side dish. If you are craving a little something sweet afterward, layer ripe bananas with vanilla Greek yogurt.

8 ounces cooked ground beef

1 (8-ounce) bag frozen mixed onions and peppers

2 (15-ounce) cans ranch-style beans, undrained

1 (15-ounce) can corn, drained

2 (10-ounce) cans tomatoes with green chiles

¼ cup chunky salsa

1 tablespoon taco seasoning

1 cup shredded Cheddar cheese, divided

1 cup corn chips, divided

¼ cup sour cream, divided

1 avocado, sliced, divided

1. In a large pot set over medium heat, stir together the beef, onions and peppers, beans, corn, tomatoes with green chiles, salsa, and taco seasoning.

2. Cook for 5 to 10 minutes, or until heated through, adding a little water if needed to thin the soup.

3. Ladle the soup into 4 bowls. Serve each topped with ¼ cup of Cheddar cheese, ¼ cup of corn chips, 1 tablespoon of sour cream, and one-quarter of the avocado slices.

TO FREEZE

1. To a large, labeled freezer-safe bag, add the beef, onions and peppers, beans, corn, tomatoes with green chiles, salsa, and taco seasoning.

2. To a small freezer-safe bag, add the Cheddar cheese. Seal the bag and slip into the large bag with the other ingredients.

3. Seal the bag, flatten, and freeze flat.

4. The night before cooking, transfer the meal from the freezer to the refrigerator to thaw overnight.

5. The next day, remove the Cheddar cheese packet. Set aside.

6. To a large pot set over medium heat, add the contents of the large bag.

7. Cook for 5 to 10 minutes, or until heated through, adding some water, if needed, to thin the soup.

8. Ladle the soup into 4 bowls. Serve each topped with ¼ cup of Cheddar cheese, ¼ cup of corn chips, 1 tablespoon of sour cream, and one-quarter of the avocado slices.

TIP: If you'd like to cut some calories and fat, use ground turkey instead of ground beef and top with reduced-fat Cheddar cheese and sour cream.

BAKED BEANS AND SAUSAGE

Serves: 4 Prep time: 5 minutes Cook time: 10 minutes

When you are looking for an all-American dinner, you can't go wrong with baked beans. This sweet, tangy combination of beans and smoked sausage is family friendly anytime. Serve with onion rings, cole slaw, and your favorite cookies for dessert. This recipe is not recommended for freezing because the beans get mushy.

1 (28-ounce) can baked beans

1 cup frozen diced onions

¼ cup dark brown sugar

2 tablespoons prepared yellow mustard

16 ounces precooked smoked sausage, sliced

1. In a medium pot over medium heat, dump in the baked beans, onions, brown sugar, mustard, and sausage. Stir to combine. Bring to a simmer.

2. Cook, for about 10 minutes, stirring occasionally to keep the mixture from sticking.

3. Serve hot.

TIP: Make this dish savory by using ranch-style beans and omitting the brown sugar and mustard. Add 2 (4-ounce) cans of diced green chiles with the sausage.

3 *Dump It in a Skillet*

A GOOD SKILLET MEAL typically means a whole meal prepared in one pan. It's like magic—everything goes in, and 10 minutes later a delicious meal comes out. You won't need much else other than a salad and bread to complete the meal.

Skillet dump meals are "dumptastically" easy. With just a good-size skillet, a burner, a recipe, and the right ingredients you can whip up dinner in no time at all. Effortless cooking at its best—the only thing easier is having a personal chef. Of course, cleanup is easy, too. With just one dish used for mixing and cooking, you'll be out of the kitchen in no time.

You've probably seen—and tried—the prepackaged skillet meals in your grocery's freezer section. Well, you can make your own by adding the ingredients to a large freezer-safe bag or vacuum-sealed bag and freezing it until you are ready to cook. Simply dump the contents of the bag into the skillet and cook it for a fraction of the cost of the prepackaged meals.

You can also use an electric skillet for these recipes, which makes them a great alternative in college dorm rooms, office kitchens, and anywhere else you don't have access to a real stove. Just put the skillet on a heatproof surface to avoid scorching or fire hazards, and follow the manufacturer's directions for use and cleaning.

CHICKEN ENCHILADA SKILLET

Serves: 4 Prep time: 5 minutes Cook time: 5 minutes

If you love chicken enchiladas, you are going to love this dish. It is quick and easy, and, while not the most beautiful dish in the world, it really is one of the tastiest. Serve with a salad and you won't need much else. If you like a sweet finish, warm ½ cup of cream of coconut (often in the cocktail mix section), spoon over vanilla ice cream, and don't forget to top it with a cherry!

Cooking spray or olive oil

12 (6-inch) corn tortillas, torn into bite-size pieces

3 cups shredded cooked chicken

1 (10-ounce) can diced tomatoes with green chiles, undrained

1 (10-ounce) can red enchilada sauce

1 (8-ounce) can tomato sauce

1 cup shredded Mexican-blend cheese, divided

1 cup diced avocado, divided

1 cup sour cream, divided

1. Spray a large skillet with cooking spray, or oil it lightly with olive oil. Place it over medium heat.

2. Add the tortillas and chicken. Stir to combine.

3. Add the tomatoes with green chiles and their liquid, enchilada sauce, tomato sauce, and ½ cup of Mexican-blend cheese. Mix well and cover.

4. Cook for about 5 minutes, stirring occasionally, or until heated through.

5. Sprinkle with the remaining ½ cup of cheese.

6. Top each serving with ¼ cup of diced avocado and ¼ cup of sour cream.

TO FREEZE

1. To a large, labeled freezer-safe bag, add the tortillas, chicken, tomatoes with green chiles and their liquid, enchilada sauce, tomato sauce, and ½ cup of Mexican-blend cheese.

2. To a small freezer-safe bag, add the remaining ½ cup of Mexican-blend cheese. Seal the bag and slip it into the large bag with the other ingredients.

3. Seal the bag, flatten, and freeze flat.

4. The night before cooking, transfer the meal from the freezer to the refrigerator to thaw overnight.

5. The next day, remove the cheese packet from the large bag. Set aside.

6. Spray a large skillet with cooking spray, or oil it lightly with olive oil. Place it over medium heat. Dump in the contents of the large bag. Stir to combine.

7. Cook for about 5 minutes, stirring occasionally, or until heated through.

8. Sprinkle with the reserved cheese.

9. Top each serving with ¼ cup of diced avocado and ¼ cup of sour cream.

TIP: If you like a creamy chicken enchilada, substitute a can of condensed cream of chicken soup and a can of condensed cream of mushroom soup for the red enchilada sauce and tomato sauce. Use pepper Jack cheese to spice it up.

SOUTHWEST CHICKEN SKILLET

Serves: 4 *Prep time:* 2 minutes *Cook time:* 15 minutes

This skillet dinner is packed with lots of big Southwest flavor—spicy jalapeños, tangy tomatoes, sweet corn, and all the other things you love about Mexican food. Fresh baby spinach leaves, mandarin orange slices, and poppy seed vinaigrette make a delicious salad that goes well with this dish. Make a quick pie with a premade graham cracker crust and lemon pie filling.

....

2 cups chicken broth

2 cups diced cooked chicken fajita meat

2 cups frozen mixed onions and peppers

1 (10-ounce) can tomatoes with green chiles

1 (15-ounce) can black beans, drained and rinsed

1 cup frozen corn

¼ cup jarred, sliced jalapeños

1 tablespoon chili powder

1 teaspoon ground cumin

½ teaspoon chipotle powder

1 cup instant rice

1 cup grated Mexican-blend cheese

¼ cup chopped fresh cilantro

....

1. To a large skillet set over high heat, add the chicken broth. Bring to a boil.

2. Add the chicken, onions and peppers, tomatoes with green chiles, black beans, corn, jalapeños, chili powder, cumin, chipotle powder, and rice. Stir to combine.

3. Return the mixture to a boil. Cover the skillet. Reduce the heat to low.

4. Cook for 10 minutes. Remove the skillet from heat. Let stand, covered, for 5 minutes more.

5. Sprinkle with the cheese and cilantro before serving.

TIP: Cooked ground beef works really well in this dish. Substitute tomato juice or beef broth for the chicken broth and follow the directions as indicated.

ITALIAN-STYLE CHICKEN AND VEGETABLES

Serves: 4 *Prep time:* 5 minutes *Cook time:* 15 minutes

When you want quick Italian food and you're tired of pasta, this Italian-Style Chicken and Vegetables is perfect. It's so packed with good-for-you veggies that you won't need anything on the side. If you want to enhance the meal, a salad and garlic bread are welcome additions. Lemon sherbet ends the meal on a refreshing note.

- -

2 cups chopped cooked chicken

1 (14-ounce) package frozen mixed onions and peppers

1 (14-ounce) can white cannellini beans, drained and rinsed

1 (14-ounce) can stewed tomatoes

1 (10-ounce) package frozen California-blend vegetables

3 tablespoons bottled minced garlic

1 tablespoon dried basil

2 teaspoons dried oregano

Grated Parmesan cheese, for garnishing (optional)

- -

1. In a large skillet set over medium heat, dump the chicken, onions and peppers, cannellini beans, tomatoes, vegetables, garlic, basil, and oregano. Bring to a simmer.

2. Cook for about 10 minutes, or until heated through.

3. Serve with a sprinkle of Parmesan (if using).

TO FREEZE

1. To a large, labeled freezer-safe bag, add the chicken, onions and peppers, cannellini beans, tomatoes, vegetables, garlic, basil, and oregano.

2. Seal the bag, flatten, and freeze flat.

3. The night before cooking, transfer the meal from the freezer to the refrigerator to thaw overnight.

4. The next day, place a large skillet over medium heat. Dump in the contents of the bag. Bring to a simmer.

5. Cook for about 10 minutes, or until heated through.

6. Serve with a sprinkle of Parmesan (if using).

TIP: Cooked Italian sausage works well in place of the chicken. Use either the spicy or sweet kind, depending on your preference.

JUST PEACHY BARBECUE CHICKEN

Serves: 4 Prep time: 2 minutes Cook time: 15 minutes

The flavor of this dish changes depending on the type of barbecue sauce you use. Add deli potato salad and cole slaw and bake some canned biscuits while the chicken is warming. Finish with red, white, and blue ice cream sundaes—vanilla ice cream with blueberries and strawberries on top.

1 cup barbecue sauce

2 teaspoons prepared yellow mustard

¼ cup peach preserves

1 rotisserie chicken, cut into pieces

1 (14.5-ounce) can sliced peaches, drained

1. In a small bowl, whisk together the barbecue sauce, mustard, and peach preserves. Set aside.

2. To a large skillet set over medium heat, add the chicken.

3. Add the barbecue sauce mixture.

4. Dump the peaches over the top.

5. Cook for about 15 minutes, or until warmed through.

TO FREEZE

1. To a large, labeled freezer-safe bag, add the barbecue sauce,

mustard, peach preserves, chicken, and peaches.

2. Seal the bag, flatten, and freeze flat.

3. The night before cooking, transfer the meal from the freezer to the refrigerator to thaw overnight.

4. The day of cooking, place a large skillet over medium heat. Dump in the contents of the bag.

5. Cook for about 15 minutes, or until warmed through.

TIP: This sweet, tangy sauce is delicious with pork roast as well. Make this a slow cooker meal by using raw chicken or pork in place of the cooked chicken and cooking all the ingredients on low for 8 hours.

ORANGE-CHICKEN SKILLET

Serves: 4 Prep time: 2 minutes Cook time: 5 minutes

Cooked chicken is coated in a sweet, slightly spicy orange sauce and served over rice. Its bright flavors make any day better. You can also serve it over quinoa, couscous, or any starch you prefer. Add some egg rolls from the freezer section and you'll have Asian takeout right at home. Dessert is easy, too, when you blend 1 (3.4-ounce) box of pistachio pudding mix with 8 ounces of whipped topping, then stir a 20-ounce can of crushed pineapple (drained), and 1 cup of mini marshmallows.

½ cup orange juice

¼ cup orange marmalade

2 tablespoons soy sauce

½ teaspoon sesame chili oil

¼ teaspoon ground ginger

¼ cup chopped mixed onions and peppers

2 cups diced cooked chicken

2 cups hot cooked rice

½ cup sliced scallions

2 tablespoons sesame seeds

1. In a large skillet set over medium heat, combine the orange juice, orange marmalade, soy sauce, sesame chili oil, and ginger. Bring to a simmer. Whisk until smooth.

2. Add the onions and peppers and chicken.

3. Stir to coat the chicken completely with the orange sauce.

4. Cook for about 5 minutes, or until warmed through.

5. Spoon over the hot rice. Sprinkle with the scallions and sesame seeds to serve.

TO FREEZE

1. To a large, labeled freezer-safe bag, add the orange juice, orange marmalade, soy sauce, sesame chili oil, ginger, onions and peppers, and chicken.

2. Seal the bag, flatten, and freeze flat.

3. The night before cooking, transfer the meal from the freezer to the refrigerator to thaw overnight.

4. The next day, place a large skillet set over medium heat. Dump in the contents of the bag.

5. Stir to coat the chicken completely with the orange sauce.

6. Cook for about 5 minutes, or until warmed through.

7. Spoon over the hot rice. Sprinkle with the scallions and sesame seeds to serve.

TIP: Diced cooked pork roast is delicious when substituted for the chicken in this recipe. To make delicious lettuce wraps, spoon the orange chicken with a little rice on romaine lettuce leaves and carefully roll up.

CHEESY SMOKED SAUSAGE AND PASTA SKILLET

Serves: 4 Prep time: 2 minutes Cook time: 15 minutes

Hearty, gooey comfort food is always a welcome meal. This dish blends tender smoky sausage and small-shaped pasta with a creamy, cheesy sauce. The pasta catches the sauce so you get all of the goodness in every bite. Applesauce makes a great side dish. The sweet apple flavor enhances the cheese. This is bound to become a family favorite. Serve with your favorite vegetable on the side, some dinner rolls, and the applesauce.

....

1½ cups diced mixed onions and peppers

2 cups chicken broth

1 (10-ounce) can diced tomatoes, undrained

½ cup half-and-half

8 ounces small pasta shells

1 pound smoked sausage, sliced

1 tablespoon bottled minced garlic

1 cup shredded mild Cheddar cheese

....

1. To a large skillet set over medium-high heat, add the onions and peppers, chicken broth, tomatoes and their liquid, half-and-half, pasta, sausage, and garlic. Bring to a boil. Cover. Reduce the heat to low.

2. Simmer for 15 minutes, or until the pasta is tender.

3. Stir in the Cheddar cheese and cover the skillet. Remove from the heat.

4. Let stand for 3 minutes and serve.

TIP: Any smoked sausage or kielbasa will work perfectly in this dish —you can even use hot dogs or diced ham. Small pasta is best, so choose shells, farfalle, fusilli, and similar shapes. If you like a smokier flavor, try smoked Gouda in place of the Cheddar.

POTATOES, SPINACH, AND KIELBASA

Serves: 4 Prep time: 2 minutes Cook time: 10 minutes

Potatoes have been filling up hungry tummies for centuries. They are delicious in this recipe because they get a little crispy, golden brown caramelization in the first few minutes of cooking. The smoky juices from the sausage coat the potatoes and spinach, while the honey mustard gives the dish a sweet, tangy flavor. Serve with crusty rye bread and coleslaw on the side. A slice of pound cake with a scoop of vanilla ice cream and warmed apple pie filling is a homey finish to the meal.

- -

2 tablespoons olive oil

2 (15-ounce) cans diced potatoes, drained

12 ounces smoked sausage, cut into ¼-inch slices

½ cup chopped onion

¼ cup honey mustard salad dressing

4 cups baby spinach

- -

1. In a large, heavy skillet set over medium heat, combine the olive oil, potatoes, sausage, and onion. Sauté for about 5 minutes, or until lightly browned.

2. Stir in the honey mustard dressing and spinach.

3. Simmer, uncovered, for about 3 minutes, or until the spinach is wilted.

TO FREEZE

1. To a large, labeled freezer-safe bag, add olive oil, potatoes, sausage, and onion.

2. Seal the bag, flatten, and freeze flat.

3. The night before cooking, transfer the meal from the freezer to the refrigerator to thaw overnight.

4. The next day, place a large, heavy skillet over medium heat. Dump in the contents of the bag.

5. Sauté for about 5 minutes, or until lightly browned.

6. Stir in the honey mustard dressing and spinach.

7. Simmer, uncovered, for about 3 minutes, or until the spinach is wilted.

TIP: Kale is increasingly popular for its healthy nutrients and delicious flavor. It makes an excellent substitute for the spinach in this recipe. Cut the kale into small pieces because it does take a little longer to cook than the tender spinach leaves.

IRISH HASH SKILLET DINNER

Serves: 4 Prep time: 5 minutes Cook time: 15 minutes

You're in luck! This quick dinner is an easy addition to your St. Patrick's Day menu or any day you want a hearty meal in minutes. Serve with multi-grain rolls and pickled beets. For dessert, make a festive green-and-white parfait by layering instant pistachio pudding with vanilla pudding and finished with whipped topping.

....

2 tablespoons olive oil

1 pound cooked ground beef

1 pound frozen diced hash brown potatoes

1 cup frozen mixed onions and peppers, thawed

1 cup beef broth

¼ cup dark beer, such as Guinness

2 tablespoons vinegar

2 tablespoons prepared yellow mustard

1 tablespoon Worcestershire sauce

4 cups cole slaw mix

4 slices precooked bacon, crumbled

....

1. In a large, heavy skillet set over medium heat, heat the olive oil for about 1 minute, or until hot.

2. Add the ground beef, potatoes, and onions and peppers.

3. Cook for about 5 minutes, or until the potatoes are lightly

browned.

4. In a small bowl, whisk together the beef broth, beer, vinegar, mustard, and Worcestershire sauce.

5. Add the cole slaw mix to the skillet. Pour in the broth mixture. Bring to a simmer.

6. Cook for 5 to 10 minutes, or until the cabbage is tender and most of the liquid has evaporated.

7. Top with the bacon and serve.

TIP: Two cups of leftover cooked roast beef or corned beef is a fantastic substitute for the ground beef in this dish. Follow the rest of the instructions as they are.

BEEF STIR-FRY

Serves: 4 *Prep time:* 2 minutes *Cook time:* 10 minutes

Stir-fry is always fast and easy, but this one beats them all. You begin with cooked beef (hint: You can even use sliced roast beef from the deli!), frozen stir-fry vegetables, and a commercial stir-fry sauce, and just warm it through. Add a few touches of your own, like cashews or sesame seeds, a scoop of hot rice, and it's ready to serve in less than 10 minutes. Make a quick dessert with vanilla instant pudding with granola sprinkled on top.

1 tablespoon sesame oil

1 pound cooked beef strips

1 (10-ounce) bag frozen stir-fry vegetables

½ cup bottled stir-fry sauce

Dash Sriracha sauce (optional)

½ cup chopped peanuts

1. To a large, heavy skillet set over high heat, add the sesame oil. Heat for 1 minute.

2. Add the beef and vegetables. Cook, stirring, for 1 to 2 minutes.

3. Add the stir-fry sauce and cover the skillet. Reduce the heat to low.

4. Simmer for about 5 minutes, or until heated through.

   Stir in Sriracha sauce (if using).

5.

6. Top with the peanuts and serve.

TO FREEZE

1. To a large, labeled freezer-safe bag, add the sesame oil, beef, vegetables, stir-fry sauce, and Sriracha (if using).

2. Seal the bag, flatten, and freeze flat.

3. The night before cooking, transfer the meal from the freezer to the refrigerator to thaw overnight.

4. The next day, place a large, heavy skillet over high heat. Dump in the contents of the bag.

5. Cook, stirring, for 1 to 2 minutes. Cover. Reduce the heat to low. Simmer for about 5 minutes, or until heated through.

6. Top with the peanuts and serve.

TIP: Chicken, pork, shrimp, or scallops—nearly anything works in this recipe. If you like more heat, use a sesame chili oil instead of the plain type. Also, stir-fry sauce can be very different from one brand to the next. Try a few until you find your favorite.

SKILLET STROGANOFF

Serves: 4 Prep time: 2 minutes Cook time: 15 minutes

Few people can resist creamy, beefy stroganoff with lots of tender noodles. Adjust the amounts of onions and mushrooms to fit your family's preferences. Warm dinner rolls and pickled beets are especially good with this meal, but a crisp salad works just as well. Fresh fruit is an easy choice to end the meal on a sweet note.

1 pound cooked ground beef

½ cup frozen mixed onions and peppers

1 teaspoon bottled minced garlic

2 cups milk

1 cup beef broth

1 teaspoon smoked paprika

Salt

Freshly ground black pepper

8 ounces egg noodles

1 (4-ounce) can sliced mushrooms, drained

1 cup sour cream

1. In a large skillet set over medium heat, combine the ground beef, onions and peppers, garlic, milk, beef broth, and paprika. Season with the salt and pepper.

2. Bring to a boil. Add the noodles. Stir to combine. Cover the skillet. Reduce the heat to low.

3. Simmer for about 10 minutes, or until the noodles are tender. If too much liquid remains, remove the cover and simmer for about 2 minutes more, or until some evaporates.

4. Add the mushrooms and sour cream. Stir gently to combine. Simmer for 1 to 2 minutes to heat through.

TIP: Cooked, sliced roast beef, pork, or chicken breast all work really well in this recipe. You can substitute low-fat milk and plain Greek yogurt for the sour cream if you want to reduce the fat.

SKILLET LASAGNA IN A FLASH

Serves: 4 Prep time: 5 minutes Cook time: 15 minutes

When you are hungry for lasagna but don't even have enough time for the frozen kind, try this quick skillet meal for all of the Italian flavor without all of the time commitment. Add a salad, some garlic bread, and gelato for dessert.

1 pound cooked ground beef or Italian sausage

1 (28-ounce) can Italian-style diced tomatoes

1 (12-ounce) package frozen mixed onions and peppers

1½ cups chicken broth

1 (8-ounce) can tomato sauce

1 tablespoon bottled minced garlic

2 (9-ounce) packages fresh cheese ravioli from the refrigerated section

8 ounces shredded mozzarella cheese

½ cup grated Parmesan cheese

1. In a large, heavy skillet set over medium heat, dump the ground beef, tomatoes, onions and peppers, chicken broth, tomato sauce, garlic, and cheese ravioli. Bring to a simmer.

2. Cook for about 15 minutes, or until the ravioli is tender and the sauce is heated through.

3. Remove from the heat. Stir in the mozzarella cheese and Parmesan cheese and serve.

TIP: Fresh pasta in the refrigerated section is an asset to any busy cook because it can be prepared so quickly. Experiment with different shapes, colors, and fillings. Fresh chicken or beef ravioli is also delicious in this recipe. If you can't find fresh you can use frozen, but you'll need to simmer it in boiling water before adding it to the recipe.

CHILI AND CORNBREAD

Serves: 4 Prep time: 5 minutes Cook time: 10 minutes

This budget- and kid-friendly meal is a twist on the classic beans and cornbread that has helped stretch so many budgets over the decades. Since you start with prepared chili, the dish is full of flavor without any real effort. Serve with a salad, and use premade brownies to fill a need for dessert.

2 (15-ounce) cans chili

1 (15-ounce) can ranch-style beans

1 (12-ounce) package frozen mixed onions and peppers

2 cups frozen corn

2 cups shredded Cheddar cheese

1 (8-inch-square) bakery cornbread, cut into 1-inch cubes

1. In a large skillet set over medium heat, combine the chili, beans, onions and peppers, and corn. Bring to a simmer and cook for 7 minutes.

2. Top with the Cheddar cheese.

3. Evenly divide the cornbread among 4 bowls.

4. Top with equal amounts of chili and serve.

TO FREEZE

1. To a large, labeled freezer-safe container, add the chili, beans,

onions and peppers, and corn.

2. To a small freezer-safe bag, add the Cheddar cheese. Seal the bag and slip it into the container with the other ingredients.

3. Seal the container and place it in the freezer.

4. The night before cooking, transfer the meal from the freezer to the refrigerator to thaw overnight.

5. The next day, remove the Cheddar cheese packet. Set aside.

6. Place a large skillet over medium heat. Dump in the content of the container. Bring to a simmer.

7. Top with the Cheddar cheese.

8. Evenly divide the cornbread among 4 bowls.

9. Top with equal amounts of chili and serve.

TIP: Use any kind of chili you prefer. If you have a few extra minutes —and are using a cast-iron or other ovenproof skillet—add the cornbread cubes to the skillet and then top with the cheese. Put the ovenproof skillet under the broiler for a few minutes to melt the cheese. Be careful; it burns quickly.

SHRIMP FRIED RICE

Serves: 4 Prep time: 2 minutes Cook time: 8 minutes

Shrimp fried rice is an almost effortless dish when you begin with prepared ingredients! You really don't need anything else with this savory one-dish meal—unless you pick up some egg rolls and keep them warm while you toss this together. Serve with lemon or lime wedges to squeeze over the top to brighten the shrimp. Need a dessert? Instant lemon pudding layered with crushed vanilla wafers is quick and delicious!

2 tablespoons sesame oil

2 large eggs, beaten

3 cups cooked rice

8 ounces peeled, deveined, and cooked shrimp

1 (8-ounce) package frozen mixed peas and diced carrots

4 ounces frozen snow peas

3 tablespoons soy sauce

½ teaspoon ground ginger

1. To a large, heavy skillet set over medium heat, add the sesame oil.

2. Pour in the beaten eggs. Cook, stirring with a spatula, for about 2 minutes, or until done.

3. Add the rice, shrimp, peas and carrots, snow peas, soy sauce, and ginger. Stir to combine.

4. Cook for about 5 minutes, stirring frequently to keep from sticking, until heated through.

TIP: This is a great dish to use up those leftovers. Corn, green beans, spinach, and water chestnuts all are delicious. Cooked chicken, pork, or beef can be used in place of the shrimp.

MEATBALLS WITH HOISIN SAUCE

Serves: 4 Prep time: 2 minutes Cook time: 10 minutes

Hoisin sauce is sweet and salty and often spiced with chiles. It brings out all kinds of flavor in meat. In this dish, prepared hoisin sauce is mixed with pineapple juice and a little sugar to give it a brighter sweetness. Use your favorite frozen meatballs, as long as they're precooked. This saucy meatball recipe is delicious over rice. Steam snow peas in the microwave with a drizzle of sesame oil for the perfect side dish. For an easy dessert, spoon whipped topping onto individual dessert plates and scoop ready-made gelatin cups atop each. Top with sliced bananas, strawberries, and fresh grapes.

- -

2 tablespoons sesame oil

16 precooked meatballs, thawed if frozen

½ cup frozen mixed onions and peppers

¼ cup pineapple chunks

2 tablespoons hoisin sauce

3 tablespoons pineapple juice

1 tablespoon brown sugar

½ cup chopped scallions

- -

1. To a large, heavy skillet set over medium heat, add the sesame oil. Heat for 1 minute.

2. Add the meatballs and onions and peppers.

3. Cook for about 5 minutes, turning frequently, until thoroughly

heated.

4. Stir in the pineapple chunks, hoisin sauce, pineapple juice, and brown sugar.

5. Simmer for 2 to 3 minutes, or until the sauce is hot.

6. Garnish with the scallions before serving.

TO FREEZE

1. To a large, labeled freezer-safe bag, add the sesame oil, meatballs, onions and peppers, pineapple chunks, hoisin sauce, pineapple juice, and brown sugar.

2. Seal the bag, flatten, and freeze flat.

3. The night before cooking, transfer the meal from the freezer to the refrigerator to thaw overnight.

4. The next day, place a large, heavy skillet over medium heat. Dump in the contents of the bag.

5. Cook for about 10 minutes, or until warmed through.

6. Garnish with the scallions before serving.

> **TIP:** Use two large spoons to turn the meatballs while heating them on all sides. There is less likelihood of breaking and crumbling. It's also a good idea to use a meat thermometer to check the temperature inside the meatballs, too. That way you don't have to cut them in half to see if they are warmed all the way through. You can use turkey meatballs, if you prefer.

ZUCCHINI, BLACK BEANS, AND RICE
VEGETARIAN

Serves: 4 Prep time: 2 minutes Cook time: 3 minutes

This spicy, Southwest-inspired vegetarian dish is one that both your family and your budget will love. And, it couldn't be easier —it takes less than 5 minutes to prep and cook this meal. Serve this mouthwatering skillet with a basket of tortilla chips and you won't need much else on the table. Keep the evening sweet with instant chocolate pudding poured into a premade chocolate crumb crust and topped with a few fresh raspberries.

1 (8-ounce) package frozen zucchini

1 (8-ounce) package frozen mixed onions and peppers

1 (15-ounce) can black beans, drained and rinsed

1 (14-ounce) can fire-roasted tomatoes, undrained

¾ cup vegetable juice cocktail

1 cup raw instant rice

¾ cup shredded pepper Jack cheese

1. To a large skillet set over medium heat, add the zucchini, onions and peppers, black beans, tomatoes and their liquid, and vegetable juice. Bring to a boil.

2. Stir in the rice.

3. Cover and remove from heat. Let stand for 7 minutes, or until all the liquid is absorbed.

4. Sprinkle with the pepper Jack cheese before serving.

> **TIP:** If your family doesn't do spicy, substitute a mild Cheddar or plain Monterey Jack cheese for the pepper Jack. On the other hand, if you do like it spicy, add 1 (4-ounce) can of drained, chopped chiles or jalapeños for that extra kick.

4 *Dump It in a Casserole*

．．．．．．．．．．．．．．

A CASSEROLE IS A MEAL baked in a large, deep dish and served in that same dish. They have been family favorites for decades, perfect for potlucks, and often contain all the components of the meal from the protein to the vegetable. In other words, since it takes very little time to prepare, casseroles are perfect for the dump technique!

To ensure your casseroles are always their best:

Thaw frozen vegetables and blot them dry before using so your finished dish isn't watery.

Thaw any frozen casseroles in the refrigerator overnight before baking.

Add a few extra minutes to the cook time when using stoneware dishes because they take a bit longer to heat up than metal.

Do not cover any made-ahead casseroles that

contain tomatoes or other acidic ingredients with aluminum foil.

CHICKEN DIVAN

Serves: 8 Prep time: 2 minutes Bake time: 20 minutes

Chicken Divan is a classic. This vintage combination of chicken, broccoli, and cheese in a creamy sauce is updated here with a crispy crumb topping. You really only need a crispy salad and some brown-and-serve rolls to make this 1950s favorite complete. No one will turn down chocolate pudding if you want dessert on the table.

Cooking spray

3 cups shredded cooked chicken breast

1 (10-ounce) package frozen broccoli, thawed

1½ cups shredded Cheddar cheese, divided

1 (10.75-ounce) can condensed cream of chicken soup

1 (10.75-ounce) can condensed cream of broccoli soup

1 cup mayonnaise

1 cup sour cream

½ teaspoon curry powder (optional)

1½ cups Japanese-style panko

1. Preheat the oven to 350°F.

2. Spray a 9-by-13-inch casserole dish with cooking spray.

3. Dump the chicken and broccoli into the prepared dish.

4. In a medium bowl, blend together 1 cup of Cheddar cheese,

cream of chicken soup, cream of broccoli soup, mayonnaise, sour cream, and curry powder (if using). Pour over the chicken and broccoli. Stir to combine. Sprinkle with the remaining ½ cup of Cheddar cheese and the bread crumbs.

5. Place the dish in the preheated oven. Bake for 20 minutes, or until warmed through and bubbly.

TIP: This dish goes together fast and freezes well—so you can save one for another day. If you freeze this dish, leave off the bread crumbs until the day you plan to serve it. Add them just before cooking.

BROCCOLI-CHICKEN CASSEROLE

Serves: 8 Prep time: 2 minutes Bake time: 45 minutes

Is there anything more comforting than pasta and cheese? This dish offers both, plus hearty chicken. If you want dessert, sandwich two oatmeal cookies together with a spoonful of canned cream cheese frosting.

....

Cooking spray

1 (10.75-ounce) can condensed cream of chicken soup

2 cups water

8 ounces small-shape pasta, uncooked

2 cups chopped broccoli, thawed if frozen

2 pounds uncooked boneless, skinless chicken breasts

1 cup halved cherry tomatoes

¾ cup shredded Parmesan cheese

....

1. Preheat the oven to 375°F.

2. Spray a 9-by-13-inch casserole dish with cooking spray.

3. In the prepared dish, dump in the cream of chicken soup, water, pasta, and broccoli. Stir ingredients together.

4. Place the chicken and tomatoes on top of the pasta and broccoli. Cover tightly with aluminum foil.

5. Place the dish in the preheated oven and bake for 40 minutes.

6. Remove the foil. Top the casserole with the Parmesan cheese.

7. Bake for an additional 5 minutes and serve.

CHICKEN POTPIE

Serves: 8 Prep time: 5 minutes Bake time: 20 minutes

This is chicken potpie for a crowd. If you don't need this much, make two smaller casseroles. You can leave one unbaked and freeze for another time. Tender chicken breast, potatoes, mushrooms, and other vegetables are mixed with a creamy gravy and topped with buttery biscuits from the refrigerator section of your store. The big, flaky biscuits work best here—they sop up more of the gravy! Serve this with coleslaw and a dessert of cherry crumble made by adding a can of cherry pie filling to a pie plate and covering it with almond granola. Bake it right alongside the potpie.

- - -

Cooking spray

2 (10-ounce) cans chicken breast or 2 cups diced cooked chicken

2 (14.5-ounce) cans sliced carrots, drained

2 (14.5-ounce) cans peas, drained

2 (14.5-ounce) cans diced potatoes, drained

1 (4-ounce) can sliced mushrooms, drained

1 (8-ounce) package frozen chopped onions

1 (10.75-ounce) can condensed cream of chicken soup

1 (10.75-ounce) can condensed cream of mushroom soup

1 (8-biscuit) can refrigerated biscuits

- - -

1. Preheat the oven to 350°F.

2. Spray a 9-by-13-inch casserole dish with cooking spray.

3. In the prepared dish, dump the chicken, carrots, peas, potatoes, mushrooms, and onions.

4. In a small bowl, mix together the cream of chicken soup and the cream of mushroom soup.

5. Add the soups to the casserole. Stir well to combine.

6. Top the casserole with the biscuits.

7. Place the casserole into the preheated oven. Bake for 20 minutes, or until the biscuits are browned and the casserole is heated through.

TO FREEZE

1. In a small bowl, mix together the cream of chicken soup and the cream of mushroom soup. Set aside.

2. In a large, labeled freezer-safe bag, dump the chicken, carrots, peas, potatoes, mushrooms, and onions.

3. Add the soups.

4. Seal the bag, flatten, and freeze flat.

5. The night before cooking, transfer the meal from the freezer to the refrigerator to thaw overnight.

6. The next day, preheat the oven to 350°F.

7. Spray a 9-by-13-inch casserole dish with cooking spray.

8. Dump the contents of the bag into the casserole dish. Stir to combine.

9. Top the casserole with the biscuits.

10. Place the casserole into the preheated oven. Bake for 20 minutes, or until the biscuits are browned and the casserole is heated through.

TIP: If you'd like individual potpies, push the biscuits into greased muffin tins to form individual crusts, fill with the chicken mixture, and bake at 375°F for 15 minutes. Let them sit for 1 to 2 minutes to firm up before removing from the pan.

CHILI PIE

Serves: 4 to 6 Prep time: 2 minutes Bake time: 15 minutes

Corn chips and chili are made for each other. They come together quickly in this fun, family-friendly meal. Diced avocado is not a traditional component of this dish, but it adds texture and flavor. Chili pie is super easy and teen approved! This dish does not freeze or store well, so don't make more than you need. Succumb to the craving for your favorite chocolate sandwich cookies for dessert.

Cooking spray

1 (10.5-ounce) bag corn chips

2 (15-ounce) cans chili

½ cup diced onion

½ cup shredded Cheddar cheese

1 cup diced avocado (optional)

1. Preheat the oven to 350°F.

2. Spray a 9-by-13-inch casserole with cooking spray. Dump the corn chips over the bottom of the casserole dish.

3. Spoon the chili on top.

4. Sprinkle with the onion and Cheddar cheese.

5. Place the dish in the preheated oven. Bake for 15 minutes, or until the cheese melts and the dish is bubbly.

6. Top with diced avocado (if using).

KING RANCH CASSEROLE

Serves: 8 Prep time: 2 minutes Bake time: 25 minutes

King Ranch Casserole is an easy dish with big Texas flavor. Chicken, corn tortillas, and lots of gooey cheese combine to create a slightly spicy, stick-to-your ribs dinner that's on the table in less than 30 minutes. Serve with a side of black beans mixed with an equal amount of corn for your own family fiesta. You can easily bake this in two pans and freeze one for later.

Dessert is easy—mix 2 (14-ounce) cans of sweetened condensed milk with ⅔ cup of lime juice and ⅓ cup of sour cream. Pour into a premade graham cracker crust, and bake for 10 minutes right along with the casserole. Remove from the oven and let stand for 15 minutes for an easy Key lime–style pie.

Cooking spray

2 cups cooked chicken fajita meat

1 cup chopped mixed onions and peppers

1 (10.75-ounce) can condensed cream of chicken soup

1 (10.75-ounce) can condensed cream of mushroom soup

2 (10-ounce) cans diced tomatoes with green chiles, drained

1 teaspoon chili powder

12 (6-inch) corn tortillas, cut into small rectangles

2 cups shredded Cheddar cheese, divided

1. Preheat the oven to 350°F.

2. Spray a 9-by-13-inch casserole dish with cooking spray.

3. In a large bowl, stir together the chicken, onions and peppers, cream of chicken soup, cream of mushroom soup, tomatoes with green chiles, chili powder, tortillas, and 1 cup of Cheddar cheese until blended.

4. Spoon into the prepared casserole dish. Sprinkle the remaining 1 cup of Cheddar cheese on top.

5. Place the casserole in the preheated oven. Bake for 20 to 25 minutes, or until the top is lightly browned around the edges and the casserole is bubbly.

TO FREEZE

1. In a medium bowl, combine the cream of chicken soup, cream of mushroom soup, and tomatoes with green chiles. Mix well. Set aside.

2. To a large, labeled freezer-safe bag, add the chicken, onions and peppers, chili powder, and 1 cup of Cheddar cheese.

3. Pour the soup and tomato mixture into the bag.

4. Seal the bag, flatten, and freeze flat.

5. The night before cooking, transfer the meal from the freezer to the refrigerator to thaw overnight.

6. The next day, preheat the oven to 350°F.

7. Spray a 9-by-13-inch casserole dish with cooking spray. Add the tortillas.

8. Dump the contents of the bag over the tortillas. Stir gently to mix.

9. Sprinkle the remaining 1 cup of Cheddar cheese on top.

10. Place the casserole in the preheated oven. Bake for 20 to 25 minutes, or until the top is lightly browned around the edges and the casserole is bubbly.

TIP: If you'd like this a little spicier, substitute 1 cup of pepper Jack cheese for half of the Cheddar cheese. Mix the two together and use as directed.

SPANISH RICE

Serves: 4 Prep time: 2 minutes Bake time: 15 minutes

Spanish rice is a versatile, toss-together meal made quickly with instant rice. It's slightly spicy and tangy, with lots of tomato flavor. Smoked paprika adds a deep, smoky flavor. Make a side dish with a spring mix bagged salad with Catalina dressing and croutons. For dessert, layer vanilla wafers in dessert cups with bananas, vanilla pudding, and whipped topping.

Cooking spray

1 pound cooked ground beef

2 cups uncooked instant rice

1 cup tomato juice

1 (10-ounce) can diced tomatoes with green chiles

1 cup diced mixed onions and peppers

1 tablespoon bottled minced garlic

½ teaspoon chili powder

½ teaspoon smoked paprika

¼ teaspoon cumin

Salt

Freshly ground black pepper

1. Preheat the oven to 350°F.

2. Spray a 9-by-13-inch pan with cooking spray.

3. Dump in the ground beef, rice, tomato juice, tomatoes with green chiles, onions and peppers, garlic, chili powder, paprika, and cumin. Season with the salt and pepper. Stir gently to combine.

4. Cover the dish with aluminum foil and place it in the preheated oven. Bake for 15 minutes.

5. Remove from the oven and let stand for 1 to 2 minutes before serving.

TIP: You can substitute smoked sausage, kielbasa, or leftover chicken or pot roast for the ground beef in this recipe. It's also good with leftover vegetables like peas, corn, carrots, or spinach added. It doesn't freeze well, but it's so quick you can make it in less time than it takes to warm a premade dish.

CREOLE CHICKEN

Serves: 8 Prep time: 2 minutes Bake time: 20 minutes

This slightly spicy, slightly sweet chicken dish has a flavor that's similar to barbecue. Serve with deli-purchased potato salad for a delicious family meal—Cajun style. For a special treat, sauté 4 sliced bananas in ¼ cup of butter and ¼ cup of brown sugar, stirring frequently. Spoon hot over vanilla ice cream. Delish!

Cooking spray

1 (14-ounce) can diced fire-roasted tomatoes, undrained

½ cup frozen mixed onions and peppers

½ cup diced celery

1 tablespoon brown sugar

1 tablespoon olive oil

2 teaspoons Worcestershire sauce

2 teaspoons red wine vinegar

1 teaspoon bottled minced garlic

½ teaspoon dried basil

¾ teaspoon Cajun seasoning, such as Tony Chachere's

½ teaspoon Tabasco sauce

2 pounds uncooked boneless, skinless chicken breasts

1. Preheat the oven to 350°F.

2. Spray a 9-by-13-inch casserole with cooking spray.

3. In a medium bowl, mix together the tomatoes and their liquid, onions and peppers, celery, brown sugar, olive oil, Worcestershire sauce, red wine vinegar, garlic, basil, Cajun seasoning, and Tabasco sauce.

4. Put the chicken in the prepared casserole dish.

5. Pour the tomato mixture on top.

6. Place the dish in the preheated oven. Bake for 20 minutes, or until the chicken registers 165°F on an instant-read meat thermometer.

TO FREEZE

1. To a large, labeled freezer-safe bag, add the chicken, tomatoes and their liquid, onions and peppers, celery, brown sugar, olive oil, Worcestershire sauce, red wine vinegar, garlic, basil, Cajun seasoning, and Tabasco sauce.

2. Seal the bag, flatten, and freeze flat.

3. The night before cooking, transfer the meal from the freezer to the refrigerator to thaw overnight.

4. The next day, preheat the oven to 350°F.

5. Spray a 9-by-13-inch casserole with cooking spray.

6. Dump the contents of the bag into the prepared dish.

7. Place the dish in the preheated oven. Bake for 20 minutes, or until the chicken registers 165°F on an instant-read meat thermometer.

TIP: This recipe also makes great Cajun pork. Use boneless pork in place of the chicken and follow the instructions as written.

FRENCH ONION MEATBALLS

Serves: 8 Prep time: 2 minutes Bake time: 25 minutes

This recipe is just about the most versatile meal you can find. Rich beef and onion flavors, just like your favorite French onion soup, are infused into the meatballs during baking. There's lots of broth in this dish, which makes it great for serving with rice or potatoes! Heat green beans for a side dish, serve rolls if you want, and for dessert, try bakery brownies with chocolate ice cream and hot fudge sauce on top. Anybody hungry?

1 (18-ounce) package frozen meatballs

1 (8-ounce) package frozen diced onions

1 (10.75-ounce) can condensed French onion soup

8 slices Swiss cheese

1. Preheat the oven to 375°F.

2. In a medium casserole dish, combine the meatballs and onions.

3. Pour in the French onion soup.

4. Cover the dish with aluminum foil and place it in the preheated oven. Bake for 20 minutes.

5. Uncover the dish. Top the meatballs with the Swiss cheese slices.

6. Continue to cook for 2 to 3 minutes more, or until the cheese melts.

TO FREEZE

1. To a large, labeled freezer-safe bag, add the meatballs, onions, and French onion soup.

2. Seal the bag, flatten, and freeze flat.

3. The night before cooking, transfer the meal from the freezer to the refrigerator to thaw overnight.

4. The next day, preheat the oven to 375°F.

5. Dump the contents of the bag into a medium casserole dish.

6. Cover the dish with aluminum foil and place it in the preheated oven. Bake for 20 minutes.

7. Uncover the dish. Top the meatballs with the Swiss cheese slices.

8. Continue to cook for 2 to 3 minutes more, or until the cheese melts.

TIP: Make French onion meatball sandwiches with this recipe by spooning the meatballs into warm hoagie rolls before topping with the cheese. Add sautéed onions, peppers, or whatever toppings you prefer. Use the broth as a dip—it's delicious. You can also make this in a slow cooker on low for 6 hours. Just leave out the cheese until you serve the meatballs. This dish freezes well after cooking, too.

CHEESEBURGER PARADISE PIE

Serves: 4 to 6 Prep time: 2 minutes Bake time: 25 minutes

These "impossible" pies became popular in the 1960s when busy home cooks were shown how to add a few ingredients to biscuit mix to create dinner in minutes. They are just as quick and easy today! Serve with an iceberg lettuce wedge drizzled with Thousand Island dressing for a classic midcentury meal. This does not freeze well, but you can keep it covered in the refrigerator for up to three days. Create sweet endings with crushed chocolate sandwich cookies folded into some instant vanilla pudding.

Cooking spray

1 pound cooked ground beef

1 cup frozen mixed onions and peppers

½ teaspoon salt

½ teaspoon garlic powder

1 teaspoon Worcestershire sauce

1 cup shredded cheese (any type you prefer)

1 cup biscuit mix

1 cup milk

2 large eggs

1. Preheat the oven to 400°F.

2. Spray a 9-inch pie pan with cooking spray.

3. In a large bowl, mix together the ground beef, onions and peppers, salt, garlic powder, and Worcestershire sauce.

4. Spoon the mixture into the prepared pie pan.

5. Sprinkle the cheese on top.

6. In a medium bowl, whisk together the biscuit mix, milk, and eggs until smooth.

7. Pour the biscuit mixture over the meat and cheese mixture.

8. Place the pan in the preheated oven. Bake for 25 minutes, or until a knife inserted in the center comes out clean.

TIP: Although American or Cheddar are the classic cheeses used in this recipe, use anything you prefer. For a delicious kick, season the meat with taco seasoning and use pepper Jack cheese.

CHEESY HAM AND TATER TOT CASSEROLE

Serves: 8 *Prep time:* 2 minutes *Bake time:* 20 minutes

Ham, potatoes, and lots of cheese in a creamy, rich sauce—what's not to love? Serve this casserole with broccoli. For dessert, try apple pie filling with crushed cinnamon graham crackers on top. Bake it right alongside the casserole and serve hot with a scoop of vanilla ice cream on the side.

Cooking spray

1½ pounds diced ham

1 (32-ounce) package frozen Tater Tots

2 (10-ounce) cans condensed cream of mushroom soup

1 cup sour cream

2 cups shredded Cheddar cheese, divided

1. Preheat the oven to 350°F.

2. Spray a 9-by-13-inch casserole dish with cooking spray.

3. Add the ham and the Tater Tots to the prepared dish. Mix gently to combine.

4. In a medium bowl, whisk together the cream of mushroom soup and sour cream until smooth.

5. Stir in 1 cup of Cheddar cheese.

6. Spoon the soup mixture over the ham and Tater Tots.

7. Sprinkle with the remaining 1 cup of Cheddar cheese.

8. Place the dish in the preheated oven. Bake for 20 minutes, or until heated through.

TIP: Cooked ground beef works well in this recipe, especially when you add 1 (4-ounce) can of chopped green chiles for a bit of Southwestern flavor. It freezes well, so you can make this in two 8-inch-square pans and freeze one for later.

BACON, POTATO, AND CHEDDAR FRITTATA

Serves: 4 Prep time: 2 minutes Bake time: 25 minutes

This easy egg dish makes a quick brunch, lunch, or dinner. It's a simple and filling meal that goes together fast when you use precooked bacon. Serve with sliced tomatoes drizzled with Italian dressing and hot biscuits with butter and honey. It doesn't freeze well, but leftovers will keep in the refrigerator for a day or so.

Cooking spray

6 slices cooked bacon, crumbled

1 (8-ounce) package frozen hash brown potatoes, thawed

½ cup frozen mixed onions and peppers

1¾ cups shredded Cheddar cheese, divided

6 large eggs

¼ cup milk

½ teaspoon salt

Freshly ground black pepper

1. Preheat the oven to 400°F.

2. Spray a 9-inch deep-dish pie pan with cooking spray.

3. Add the bacon, hash browns, onions and peppers, and 1 cup of Cheddar cheese to the prepared pan.

4. In a medium bowl, whisk together the eggs, milk, and salt. Season with the pepper.

5. Pour the egg mixture over the hash browns mixture.

6. Place the pan in the preheated oven. Bake for 20 minutes.

7. Remove from the oven and sprinkle with the remaining ¾ cup of Cheddar cheese.

8. Return the casserole to the oven. Bake for 5 more minutes, or until the cheese melts.

9. Remove from the oven. Let stand for 5 minutes before serving.

TIP: Swiss cheese is a tasty substitute for the Cheddar in this recipe. You can also easily make this into a quiche by only using half the potatoes, doubling the milk, and pouring it into a frozen, unbaked piecrust. Bake until set, about 25 minutes.

PIZZA CASSEROLE

Serves: 4 Prep time: 5 minutes Bake time: 25 minutes

Homemade pizza the easy way! This recipe uses canned biscuits for the crust topped with all of your favorite toppings. In less than a half hour, you'll be sitting down to pizza. Serve with a raw vegetable tray from the grocery produce section for an easy finger-food meal that feels like the weekend any day of the week. Serve scoops of your favorite ice cream for dessert for a genuine pizza parlor feel.

Cooking spray

1 (8-biscuit) can refrigerated biscuits, quartered

1 (14-ounce) can pizza sauce

½ pound cooked ground beef

¼ pound mini pepperoni slices

1 cup frozen mixed onions and peppers

1 (10-ounce) can black olives, drained

1 (4.5-ounce) can sliced mushrooms, drained

½ cup shredded mozzarella cheese

½ cup shredded provolone cheese

1. Preheat the oven to 350°F.

2. Spray a 9-by-13-inch casserole dish with cooking spray.

3. Cover the bottom of the prepared dish with the biscuits.

4. Spread the pizza sauce over the biscuits.

5. Top with the ground beef, pepperoni, onions and peppers, olives, and mushrooms.

6. Place the dish into the preheated oven. Bake for 20 minutes, or until the biscuits are done.

7. Top with the mozzarella and provolone cheeses. Bake for 5 minutes more, or until the cheese is melted and bubbly.

8. Remove from the oven. Let stand for 5 minutes before serving.

TO FREEZE

1. In a large, labeled freezer-safe bag, combine the pizza sauce, ground beef, pepperoni, onions and peppers, olives, and mushrooms.

2. Seal the bag, flatten, and freeze flat.

3. The night before cooking, transfer the meal from the freezer to the refrigerator to thaw overnight.

4. The next day, preheat the oven to 350°F.

5. Spray a 9-by-13-inch casserole dish with cooking spray.

6. Cover the bottom of the prepared dish with the biscuits.

7. Spread the contents of the bag over the biscuits.

8. Place the dish into the preheated oven. Bake for 20 minutes, or until the biscuits are done.

9. Top with the mozzarella and provolone cheeses. Bake for 5 minutes more, or until the cheese is melted and bubbly.

10. Remove from the oven. Let stand for 5 minutes before serving.

TIP: Make individual pizza cups by pressing the biscuits into greased muffin tins to form shells. Fill with your desired toppings and bake. Sprinkle with cheese during the last few minutes. Flash freeze them on a cookie sheet by placing them in a freezer container until solid. Once frozen, you have a quick, on-the-go handheld meal when you need it. Simply microwave the pizza cup on high for about 1 minute straight from the freezer.

CRAB AND SHRIMP DELIGHT

Serves: 4 to 6 Prep time: 5 minutes Bake time: 40 minutes

If your family enjoys seafood, then this creamy crab and shrimp mixture is bound to find its way to your table often. While quick and easy, do take a few minutes to check the crab for pieces of shell. Serve with hot garlic bread and a crisp romaine lettuce salad dressed with a simple vinaigrette. A lemon pound cake from the bakery is the perfect ending.

Cooking spray

1 (10-ounce) can condensed cream of shrimp soup

1 cup milk

1 cup mayonnaise

1 (4-ounce) can crabmeat, picked over to remove any shells

1 (4-ounce) can medium shrimp

8 ounces uncooked small shell pasta

8 ounces shredded Cheddar cheese

1 (6-ounce) can French-fried onions

1. Preheat the oven to 350°F.

2. Spray a 9-by-13-inch casserole dish with cooking spray.

3. In a large bowl, whisk together the cream of shrimp soup, milk, and mayonnaise until smooth.

4. Stir in the crabmeat, shrimp, and pasta.

5. Spoon the mixture into the prepared casserole dish.

6. Sprinkle with the Cheddar cheese.

7. Cover with aluminum foil and place the dish in the preheated oven. Bake for 30 minutes.

8. Uncover and sprinkle with the French-fried onions.

9. Return to the oven and bake for 10 minutes more.

10. Serve hot.

TIP: This dish can be frozen, unbaked, as long as you omit the French-fried onions. Just put all the ingredients in a freezer-safe bag and freeze. Thaw overnight in the refrigerator and dump it into the casserole dish when ready to bake. It doesn't get easier!

NO-BOIL MAC AND CHEESE

Serves: 8 Prep time: 5 minutes Bake time: 30 minutes

Tender pasta and gooey cheese are at their best when baked until the edges are browned and crispy and the cheese clings to each piece of pasta. This variation is so easy—just toss it all in the casserole dish without even cooking the pasta! Serve with buttered green beans on the side. For dessert? Graham crackers sandwiched together with canned cream cheese frosting.

. . . .

¼ cup (½ stick) unsalted butter

2½ cups uncooked elbow macaroni

3 cups shredded Cheddar cheese

8 ounces processed cheese, cubed

4 cups milk

1 teaspoon salt

Pinch freshly ground black pepper

1 cup Japanese-style panko bread crumbs

. . . .

1. Preheat the oven to 400°F.

2. Put the butter into a 9-by-13-inch pan and into the oven just to melt.

3. Remove the pan from oven. Pour in the macaroni, stirring to make sure it's all coated with the butter.

4. Add the Cheddar cheese and processed cheese. Stir gently to

combine.

5. Carefully pour the milk over the top. Add the salt and season with the pepper. Do not stir.

6. Cover the dish with aluminum foil and place it in the preheated oven. Bake for 20 minutes.

7. Carefully remove the foil. Sprinkle with the bread crumbs and bake, uncovered, for 10 minutes more, or until the pasta is tender.

8. Remove from the oven. Let stand for 10 minutes before serving.

TIP: This dish can be frozen, uncooked, in a freezer-safe bag, and then thawed overnight and dumped into a casserole dish when you are ready to bake it. Since the liquid will soak into the pasta, it will probably be ready about 10 minutes sooner if you do it this way.

MEXICAN BAKED EGGS
VEGETARIAN

Serves: 4 to 6 Prep time: 5 minutes Bake time: 10 minutes

This spicy Southwestern vegetarian dish is quick and easy anytime of the day. Serve with warm flour tortillas, sour cream, and diced avocado. Broiled grapefruit halves with brown sugar on top are a nice accompaniment. If you don't like grapefruit, orange slices are good, too.

2 (14.5-ounce) cans diced fire-roasted tomatoes

1 (16-ounce) jar salsa

1 cup black beans, drained and rinsed

½ cup frozen corn

¼ cup chopped fresh cilantro

1 tablespoon bottled minced garlic

1 teaspoon cumin

8 large eggs

½ cup shredded Mexican-blend or Cheddar cheese

1. Preheat the oven to 375°F.

2. In a large mixing bowl, combine the tomatoes, salsa, black beans, corn, cilantro, garlic, and cumin.

3. To a 9-by-13-inch pan, add the bean mixture.

4. With the back of a spoon, make a small well in the mixture. Carefully crack 1 egg into it. Repeat with the remaining eggs.

5. Place the pan in the preheated oven. Bake for 7 to 10 minutes, or until the eggs are just set.

6. Remove from the oven. Sprinkle with the Mexican-blend cheese and serve.

TIP: If you'd like to freeze this, combine all the ingredients, except the eggs and cheese, and ladle into a freezer-safe bag. Seal the bag, flatten, and freeze flat. Thaw overnight and proceed with the recipe as written.

5 *Dump It on a Sheet Pan*

. . . .

AS YOU'VE DISCOVERED BY NOW, dump dinners can be made a variety of ways—even on a sheet pan. In this chapter you'll find all kinds of quick meals—like pizza and nachos—that can be put together fast and cooked on a sheet pan. Some of the components can be made ahead and frozen, but these recipes are generally so quick to prepare that there really isn't any reason to do so. Check the recipe tips for ideas to make them faster and easier or how to vary them from time to time. There are many types and weights of sheet pans. Choose a heavy pan with sides, which hold in any juices created during baking. A heavier pan heats more evenly and prevents scorching and burning.

Pizzas can be made with different bases. Most grocers sell pre-baked crusts, but let your imagination be your guide. French bread, English muffins, bagels, and other bakery items work just as well. Keep some staple ingredients like French fries, Tater Tots, and other starchy sides in your freezer. You can always dump a can of chili over them, add some grated cheese, and create a meal in moments. It really is that easy.

PEPPERONI FRENCH BREAD PIZZA

Serves: 4 to 6 Prep time: 5 minutes Bake time: 10 minutes

If you love pizza with a thick crust, this French bread pizza is for you. The crust is made with a loaf of French bread—thick and chewy. Use a canned tomato sauce and shredded mozzarella to create the fastest pizza ever. Add pepperoncini peppers and black olives to a bag of Caesar salad and choose fresh fruit for dessert.

....

1 loaf bakery French bread, halved lengthwise

1 (15-ounce) can pizza sauce

2 cups shredded mozzarella cheese

1 (3.5-ounce) package pepperoni

¼ cup olive oil (optional)

....

1. Preheat the oven to 425°F.

2. On a baking sheet, place the two loaf halves crust-side down.

3. Spread one-half of the pizza sauce over each piece of bread.

4. Sprinkle with the mozzarella cheese.

5. Top with the pepperoni.

6. Place the sheet in the preheated oven. Bake for about 10 minutes, or until the cheese melts.

   Remove from oven and drizzle with the olive oil (if using).

7.

8. Let stand for 1 to 2 minutes so the cheese firms up before cutting.

TIP: Be sure to use a thick, flavorful sauce or it can get lost in all of the bread. The thick crust allows you to pile on those toppings—so go ahead, add everything you like. A sourdough baguette is a nice change—it gives a tangy flavor to the pizza.

VEGETARIAN PIZZA
VEGETARIAN

Serves: 4 to 6 Prep time: 2 minutes Bake time: 10 minutes

Most grocers carry prebaked pizza crusts, usually found in the bread aisle or deli. You'll only need to add the toppings and warm until the cheese melts. In fact, it's even easier than the Pepperoni French Bread Pizza (<u>here</u>) because you don't even have to slice the bread! Serve with a big, crispy salad for a real pizzeria-style meal. Set out a variety of ice creams and toppings for a fun make-your-own sundae dessert bar.

1 (12-inch) prebaked pizza crust

1 (4-ounce) can pizza sauce

1 (8-ounce) package frozen mixed onions and peppers, thawed

1 (14-ounce) can diced tomatoes with green chiles, drained

½ cup fresh baby spinach

1 (4-ounce) can sliced black olives, drained

1 (4-ounce) can sliced mushrooms, drained

2 cups shredded mozzarella cheese

1. Preheat the oven to 450°F.

2. On a baking sheet, place the crust.

3. Spread the pizza sauce over the crust, leaving a 1-inch border all around.

4. Top with the onions and peppers, tomatoes with green chiles,

spinach, black olives, and mushrooms.

5. Sprinkle the mozzarella cheese over the toppings.

6. Place the sheet in the preheated oven. Bake for 10 minutes, or until the cheese melts and begins to brown.

7. Remove from the oven. Let stand for 1 to 2 minutes before serving.

TIP: Pizza is a great choice for entertaining. The baked crusts come in a variety of sizes so you can provide guests with individual crusts and a variety of toppings to make their own. It's a great way to prepare food for a sleepover, too!

BARBECUE CHICKEN PIZZA

Serves: 4 to 6 Prep time: 5 minutes Bake time: 10 minutes

This pizza brings together two family favorites into one perfect bite. A whole-wheat crust is the foundation of choice because of the other strong flavors involved, but you can use any crust you prefer. Serve with prepared coleslaw. For dessert, choose your favorite bakery pie while you are picking up the chicken.

. . . .

1 (12-inch) prebaked whole-wheat pizza crust

½ cup barbecue sauce

6 ounces grilled chicken, or prepared barbecued chicken

4 ounces frozen mixed onions and peppers, thawed

1½ cups shredded mozzarella cheese

½ cup shredded Cheddar cheese

. . . .

1. Preheat the oven to 450°F.

2. On a baking sheet, place the crust.

3. Spread the barbecue sauce over the crust, leaving a 1-inch border all around.

4. Distribute the chicken and onions and peppers evenly over the sauce.

5. Top with the mozzarella cheese and Cheddar cheese.

6. Place the sheet in the preheated oven. Bake for 10 minutes, or until the cheese melts and begins to brown.

7. Remove from the oven and let stand for 1 to 2 minutes before serving.

TIP: There are specialty perforated pizza pans and pizza stones that will help you achieve a crispier texture on a prebaked pizza crust. They are available at most variety stores that sell kitchen equipment. If you'd like a more homemade texture to your crust, look in the deli for unbaked pizza dough. You may also be able to buy it from your local pizzeria. It will add a few minutes to the process because you'll need to roll it out. If you like that soft, chewy crust, though, it will be worth it.

ROASTED ONIONS AND POTATOES WITH CHICKEN

Serves: 4 to 6 Prep time: 2 minutes Bake time: 35 minutes

Roasting vegetables brings out a depth of flavor and sweetness that you can't get any other way. Roasted onions are a creamy, sweet accompaniment to the chicken and potatoes. The Italian dressing adds the necessary oil for roasting as well as a tangy, garlicky flavor. Add a squeeze of fresh lemon juice over the top just before serving. Brown-and-serve rolls and steamed broccoli complete the meal. For dessert, add peach pie filling to a pie plate, top with canned biscuits, and bake. Serve with vanilla ice cream.

. . . .

2 pounds bone-in chicken breasts with skin on

1½ pounds small (golf ball-size) red potatoes, scrubbed

4 small yellow onions, unpeeled, tops removed

½ cup Italian salad dressing

. . . .

1. Preheat the oven to 400°F.

2. In a large bowl, combine the chicken, potatoes, onions, and Italian dressing. Stir to coat evenly.

3. Dump the ingredients onto a baking sheet.

4. Put the sheet in the preheated oven. Roast for 35 minutes, or until the chicken reaches 165°F in the center and the vegetables are tender.

TIP: If you prefer, substitute olive oil for the Italian dressing. Add a packet of dry ranch dressing mix to the olive oil before combining with other ingredients.

NACHOS SUPREME

Serves: 4 to 6 Prep time: 5 minutes Cook time: 5 minutes

Nachos might seem like junk food, but they can actually be fairly healthy. Meat, cheese, and vegetables are piled on top of crispy tortilla chips and baked until they are a gooey, melty perfection. Although you don't need any sides, a bowl of guacamole is a nice addition.

8 ounces tortilla chips

4 ounces diced cooked beef fajita meat

1 (15.5-ounce) can refried beans

1 (4-ounce) can sliced black olives, drained

1 (4-ounce) can sliced jalapeños, drained

1 cup shredded Cheddar cheese

1 cup salsa

1. Preheat the broiler to high.

2. On a baking sheet, spread out the tortilla chips.

3. Cover the chips with the fajita meat, refried beans, olives, and jalapeños.

4. Sprinkle with the Cheddar cheese.

5. Place the sheet under the broiler. Cook until the cheese is melted and bubbly.

6. Remove from the oven.

7. Spoon the salsa randomly over the top before serving.

TIP: You can use any cooked meat in this dish. Shrimp, grilled chicken, taco meat, or pulled pork are all delicious possibilities. If you are following a low-carb diet, you can use pork rinds in place of the tortilla chips. Omit the beans and you'll have a delicious plate of nachos without going over your carbohydrate limit for the day.

IRISH NACHOS

Serves: 4 to 6 Prep time: 5 minutes Bake time: 15 minutes

Irish Nachos are a relative newcomer to the world of great bar food, but are growing in popularity. Instead of tortilla chips, the base for Irish Nachos is potatoes—in this case, waffle fries. Corned beef is the most common topping, but you can certainly use bacon if you like.

- -

1½ pounds frozen waffle fries

½ pound chopped corned beef, or 1 (12-ounce) can corned beef, or ½ pound crumbled cooked bacon

1 cup diced onion

2 cups shredded Cheddar cheese

Chopped scallions, for garnish

Sour cream, for garnish

- -

1. Preheat the oven according to the package instructions for the waffle fries.

2. On a baking sheet, spread out the fries in a single layer.

3. Scatter the corned beef and onion over the top.

4. Place the sheet in the preheated oven. Bake for 10 minutes, or until the waffle fries are almost done.

5. Cover with the Cheddar cheese. Bake for about 5 minutes more, or until the cheese melts.

6. Sprinkle with scallions over the top. Serve with dollops of sour cream on top.

TIP: While the canned corned beef is certainly the easiest way to go with this recipe, it isn't necessarily the most flavorful. One easy way to use higher-quality corned beef without taking forever to prep is to buy ½ pound of sliced corned beef from the deli. Roll up the slices and quickly slice the tube of meat to create ¼-inch-wide strips. Use these to cover the potatoes.

SHIPWRECKED FRENCH FRIES

Serves: 4 to 6 Prep time: 5 minutes Bake time: 15 minutes

This is a messy dish—not a great finger food—but absolutely delicious and lots of fun. French fries make the base and are topped with chili, cheese, onions, peppers, and pretty much anything else you like. Serve with a scoop of coleslaw. Finish the meal with a slice of angel food cake topped with a spoonful of blueberry pie filling and a dollop of whipped cream.

1 pound frozen French fries

2 (15-ounce) cans chili with beans

1½ cups shredded Cheddar cheese

½ cup shredded pepper Jack cheese

4 ounces frozen mixed onions and peppers, thawed

1. Preheat the oven to 425°F.

2. On a baking sheet, spread out the fries in a single layer.

3. Place the sheet in the preheated oven. Bake for 10 minutes. Remove from the oven.

4. Dump the chili, Cheddar cheese, pepper Jack cheese, and onions and peppers over the top.

5. Return to the oven and bake for 5 minutes more, or until heated through.

TIP: You can use Tater Tots instead of French fries for this dish. If you really want to get crazy, substitute crispy onion rings for the French fries.

OVEN FAJITAS

Serves: 4 to 6 Prep time: 5 minutes Broil time: 5 minutes

Fajitas are a combination of grilled meats and vegetables served smoking hot on warm flour tortillas. They are most often grilled, but they don't have to be! You can roast the fajita filling in the oven. Serve with diced avocado, guacamole, sour cream, shredded cheese, and tortillas. Make a quick dessert by putting a layer of tortilla chips in a baking dish and covering with caramel sauce, chocolate chips, and pecans. Warm in the oven until it's all melted together, about 5 minutes. Watch it carefully, though!

. . . .

1 pound cooked preseasoned chicken or beef fajita meat

1 pound frozen mixed onions and peppers

8 (6-inch) flour tortillas

2 cups shredded Cheddar cheese, divided

1 cup sour cream, divided

2 cups shredded lettuce, divided

1 cup guacamole or diced avocado, divided

Salsa, for garnish

. . . .

1. Preheat the broiler to high.

2. On a baking sheet, dump together the fajita meat and onions and peppers.

3. Place the sheet under the broiler for about 5 minutes, watching carefully, until the ingredients are hot and begin to blacken in

some places. Don't let them burn.

4. Remove from oven.

5. Wrap the tortillas in a damp towel and place in the microwave. Heat on high for 1 minute, or until warm and flexible.

6. Serve accompanied by the Cheddar cheese, sour cream, lettuce, guacamole, and salsa.

TIP: You can make these ahead of time. Fill the tortillas with the cooked meat mixture, wrap tightly in plastic wrap, seal in a freezer-safe container, and freeze for quick, individual meals. Omit the sour cream, lettuce, and other toppings, though. They won't freeze well. When you need a quick, single-serving meal, remove one from the freezer and microwave on high for 2 minutes, or until hot.

OVEN-BAKED PARMESAN TILAPIA AND ROASTED CAULIFLOWER

Serves: 4 to 6 Prep time: 5 minutes Cook time: 6 minutes broiled or 20 minutes baked

Tilapia is a very mild-flavored fish that is a good starter seafood for families that don't usually serve it but want to follow a healthier diet. It broils quickly and easily right along with the cauliflower. Serve with lemon slices, a big salad, garlic bread, and some fresh fruit for dessert.

Olive oil, for oiling the pan and the cauliflower

2 pounds tilapia fillets

1 (16-ounce) bag frozen cauliflower, thawed

2 tablespoons freshly squeezed lemon juice

½ cup grated Parmesan cheese

½ cup sour cream

1 teaspoon seasoned salt

1. Preheat the broiler to high. (See recipe tip for baking instructions.)

2. Oil the baking sheet.

3. On the prepared sheet, lay the fillets and cauliflower in a single layer, and brush with the lemon juice.

4. Brush the cauliflower with the olive oil.

5. In a small bowl, mix together the Parmesan cheese, sour cream, and seasoned salt. Set aside.

6. Place the sheet in the oven. Broil the tilapia for about 3 minutes, or until the fish flakes easily with a fork.

7. Remove the sheet from the oven. Spread the cheese mixture over the fillets.

8. Broil for about 3 minutes more.

TIP: To bake rather than broil, preheat the oven to 400°F. Top the fish with the Parmesan mixture before baking. Bake for 15 to 20 minutes, or until the fish is done. Other firm-flesh fish can be used in this dish. It's especially good with red snapper.

ROASTED MIXED VEGETABLES
VEGETARIAN

Serves: 4 to 6 Prep time: 5 minutes Bake time: 1 hour

Roasted vegetables are a versatile side dish or an excellent main dish when you add a protein. They do take 1 hour to cook, but it is completely hands-off time. Although this recipe works well as part of a vegetarian meal, it is also delicious served with roast chicken, fish, or beef. Make an extravagant dessert with pound cake cut into 4 layers. Lay a slice of cake on a plate, top with whipped topping, cover with fresh berries, and add another cake layer. Repeat until all the layers are used, ending with cake.

....

Olive oil, for greasing the pan

4 cups baby carrots

2 cups raw cauliflower florets

1 cup sliced green, yellow, or red bell peppers

1 cup diced onion

2 tablespoons olive oil

1 teaspoon seasoned salt

....

1. Preheat the oven to 425°F.

2. Grease a large baking sheet with olive oil.

3. To the prepared sheet, add the carrots, cauliflower, bell peppers, and onion. Brush with additional oil.

4. Sprinkle with the seasoned salt.

5. Place the sheet in the oven. Bake for 1 hour, or until the vegetables begin to brown and are tender.

TIP: Try all types of vegetables in this dish. Beets, corn, zucchini, and mushrooms are all delicious additions.

6 *Dump It in a Slow Cooker*

· · · · · · · · · · · · ·

THE SLOW COOKER has to be one of the most valuable kitchen appliances in the known universe. You just add ingredients, set the heat and time, and go about your business. When you're ready, dinner is, too. It couldn't be easier, or could it?

Well, actually, yes. With these dump dinner recipes, it can. Imagine a busy morning when all you have to do to prepare dinner is open a bag, dump the contents into the slow cooker, turn it on, and go. Of course, you do need to put them together ahead of time, but that's super easy. Take an hour or so on a Sunday afternoon and assemble several meals. Place in vacuum-sealed or freezer-safe bags, and you've just ensured that, a few days each month, dinner is as simple as it can be— making a sandwich takes more effort than this.

Remember to label the freezer containers with the contents, date, and any special instructions. Now just fill and freeze. You'll never have to wonder whether you are thawing chicken or a family member's fishing bait again. Always thaw the contents overnight in the refrigerator before cooking. It's better for the dish and the slow cooker, too.

SOUTHWEST CHICKEN

Serves: 4 Prep time: 5 minutes Cook time: 8 hours, 10 minutes

Warm Southwestern flavors abound in this easy chicken dish. Salsa adds the majority of the flavor, so use one you like with a heat level you prefer. Stretch this dish even further by increasing the amount of beans and corn. Garnish with a little sour cream and diced avocado, if you wish. Serve with warm tortillas, butter, and a crisp salad on the side or over hot rice. If you'd like to finish with something sweet, buy bakery brownies and warm them. Serve with a scoop of dulce de leche or butter pecan ice cream with hot fudge sauce drizzled on top. Olé!

- -

1 pound boneless, skinless chicken breasts or thighs

1 (16-ounce) jar chunky salsa

1 (15-ounce) can black beans, drained and rinsed

1 cup canned or frozen corn

1 cup shredded Mexican-blend cheese

- -

1. In a slow cooker, dump the chicken, salsa, black beans, and corn.

2. Cook on low for 8 hours.

3. Using two forks, shred the chicken in the cooker.

4. Add the Mexican-blend cheese.

5. Cover. Cook for 10 minutes more, or until the cheese melts.

1. To a large, labeled freezer-safe bag, add the chicken, salsa, black beans, and corn.

2. To a smaller, freezer-safe bag, add the Mexican-blend cheese. Seal the bag and slip inside the large bag with the rest of the ingredients.

3. Seal the bag, flatten, and freeze flat.

4. The night before cooking, transfer the meal from the freezer to the refrigerator to thaw overnight.

5. The next morning, remove the cheese packet from the bag. Set aside.

6. In the slow cooker, dump the contents of the bag.

7. Cook on low for 8 hours.

8. Using two forks, shred the chicken in the cooker.

9. Add the cheese.

10. Cover. Cook for 10 minutes more, or until the cheese melts.

TIP: If you like creamy Mexican food, stir in ½ cup of heavy cream just before adding the cheese. The cream mellows out the spicy Southwestern tomato flavor. If you like a little more kick, substitute pepper Jack cheese for the Cheddar.

SWEET ORANGE-GINGER CHICKEN

Serves: 4 Prep time: 5 minutes Cook time: 8 hours

Spicy, sweet orange-ginger chicken is so easy when made in a slow cooker. Use sesame chili oil if you like it hot or regular sesame oil if you like a milder dish. While cooking, it fills the house with the most amazing aromas. Serve with hot rice, egg rolls from the deli or freezer section, and instant vanilla pudding flavored with a little almond extract or amaretto.

½ **cup honey-barbecue sauce**

½ **cup orange marmalade**

¼ **cup orange juice**

2 tablespoons soy sauce

1 teaspoon ground ginger

1 tablespoon sesame chili oil or plain sesame oil

2 pounds boneless, skinless chicken breasts or thighs

1. In a medium bowl, whisk together the barbecue sauce, marmalade, orange juice, soy sauce, ginger, and sesame oil.

2. To a slow cooker, add the chicken. Pour the sauce over the top.

3. Cook on low for 8 hours.

TO FREEZE

1. In a large, labeled freezer-safe bag, place the chicken.

2. In a medium bowl, whisk together the barbecue sauce, marmalade, orange juice, soy sauce, ginger, and sesame oil. Pour into the bag over the chicken.

3. Seal the bag, flatten, and freeze flat.

4. The night before cooking, transfer the meal from the freezer to the refrigerator to thaw overnight.

5. The next morning, dump the contents of the bag into the slow cooker.

6. Cook on low for 8 hours.

TIP: If you happen to find boneless pork roast on sale, you can substitute it for the chicken. You don't need to cut it up, but you'll want to cook it for the full 8 hours, or up to 10 hours if needed.

HONEY-CHIPOTLE CHICKEN SLIDERS

Serves: 4 to 6 Prep time: 5 minutes Cook time: 8 hours

Sweet and spicy, tender and juicy—these sliders are perfect for football get-togethers. Serve with honey mustard, fries, and some creamy coleslaw for an easy dinner—paper plates welcome! For bigger appetites, slice a bakery sourdough baguette in half, lengthwise, and warm it in the oven. Add big spoonfuls of the chicken for a hoagie that will beat anything you've had at the deli! Strawberry ice cream sandwiched between bakery sugar cookies make a refreshing dessert.

. . . .

¼ cup honey

3 tablespoons teriyaki sauce

3 tablespoons vinegar

2 tablespoons bottled minced garlic

2 tablespoons chipotles in adobo, mashed

1 tablespoon ketchup

1 pound boneless, skinless chicken breast or thighs

8 slider buns

. . . .

1. In a medium bowl, whisk together the honey, teriyaki sauce, vinegar, garlic, chipotles in adobo, and ketchup.

2. To the slow cooker, add the chicken.

3. Pour the chipotle sauce over the top.

4. Cook on low for 7 hours.

5. Using two forks, shred the chicken in the cooker. Re-cover and cook for 1 hour more.

6. Serve in the slider buns.

TO FREEZE

1. In a medium bowl, whisk together the honey, teriyaki sauce, vinegar, garlic, chipotles in adobo, and ketchup.

2. To a large, labeled freezer-safe bag, add the chicken.

3. Pour the chipotle sauce over the top.

4. Seal the bag, flatten, and freeze flat.

5. The night before cooking, transfer the meal from the freezer to the refrigerator to thaw overnight.

6. The next morning, dump the contents of the bag into the slow cooker.

7. Cook on low for 7 hours.

8. Using two forks, shred the chicken in the cooker. Re-cover and cook for 1 hour more.

9. Serve in the slider buns.

TIP: If you can't find canned chipotles in adobo (look in the Mexican foods section in your grocery store), use ½ teaspoon chipotle powder instead. Adjust the amount according to the heat level you prefer. You can substitute pork for the chicken in this recipe.

WHITE CHICKEN CHILI

Serves: 4 to 6 Prep time: 5 minutes Cook time: 8 hours

This white chicken chili is a delicious variation on regular chili. It's serious comfort food on a cold, wintery day. Its creamy texture is achieved by the long, slow cooking and the addition of dairy products at the end. The flavor is reminiscent of sour cream chicken enchiladas. Serve with corn chips or cornbread and a salad on the side. If your sweet tooth is active, spoon warm cherry pie filling over Twinkies for the easiest dessert on the planet.

¾ pound boneless, skinless chicken breast

1 teaspoon chili powder

1 teaspoon ground cumin

1 teaspoon garlic powder

¾ cup chicken broth

1 (4.5-ounce) can chopped green chiles

1 cup fresh, frozen, or canned corn

1 (15.5-ounce) can white beans, drained and rinsed

1 cup chopped onion

2 tablespoons unsalted butter

½ cup half-and-half

4 ounces cream cheese

¼ cup sour cream

1 cup shredded pepper Jack cheese

Chopped fresh cilantro, for garnishing

1. To the slow cooker, add the chicken.

2. Dump in the chili powder, cumin, garlic powder, chicken broth, green chiles, corn, white beans, and onion.

3. Cook on low for 7 hours.

4. Using two forks, shred the chicken in the cooker.

5. In a medium saucepan set over medium heat, whisk together the butter, half-and-half, cream cheese, and sour cream until smooth. Add to the slow cooker. Re-cover and cook for 1 more hour.

6. Sprinkle with the pepper Jack cheese and garnish with cilantro.

TO FREEZE

1. To a large, labeled freezer-safe bag, add the chicken, chili powder, cumin, garlic powder, chicken broth, green chiles, corn, white beans, and onion.

2. Seal the bag, flatten, and freeze flat.

3. The night before cooking, transfer the meal from the freezer to the refrigerator to thaw overnight.

4. The next morning, dump the contents of the bag into the slow cooker.

5. Cook on low for 7 hours.

6. Using two forks, shred the chicken in the cooker.

7. In a medium saucepan set over medium heat, whisk together the

butter, half-and-half, cream cheese, and sour cream until smooth. Add to the slow cooker. Re-cover and cook for 1 more hour.

8. Sprinkle with the pepper Jack cheese and garnish with cilantro.

> **TIP:** If you'd like to cut back on the fat, replace the half-and-half, cream cheese, and sour cream with skim milk, nonfat cream cheese, and fat-free sour cream, respectively.

HAWAIIAN CHICKEN

Serves: 4 Prep time: 5 minutes Cook time: 8 hours

Sweet and savory, this Hawaiian chicken is delicious over rice or on a Hawaiian bread roll to make pulled chicken sliders. A salad is always a good accompaniment. Looking for a quick dessert? A pineapple dump cake is perfect! If you like your food on the spicy side, add 1 (4-ounce) can of drained jalapeños. It adds that sweet and spicy flavor that is so delicious, even if it isn't exactly traditional!

1 pound boneless, skinless chicken thighs or breasts

2 (15-ounce) cans pineapple chunks in juice, undrained

1 (8-ounce) package frozen mixed onions and peppers

3 tablespoons brown sugar

¼ cup soy sauce

1. In a slow cooker, dump the chicken, pineapple, onions and peppers, brown sugar, and soy sauce.

2. Cook on low for 8 hours.

TO FREEZE

1. To a large, labeled freezer-safe bag, add the chicken, pineapple, onions and peppers, brown sugar, and soy sauce.

2. Seal the bag, flatten, and freeze flat.

3. The night before cooking, transfer the meal from the freezer to

the refrigerator to thaw overnight.

4. The next morning, dump the contents of the bag into the slow cooker.

5. Cook on low for 8 hours.

TIP: You don't have to use boneless chicken. You can use cut-up chicken parts, drumsticks, wings, or whatever you like. This is another recipe that works well with boneless pork roast.

CLASSIC STEW

Serves: 4 to 6 Prep time: 5 minutes Cook time: 8 hours

Every culture has some sort of stew recipe. This is the American classic with beef and lots of vegetables. A fun way to serve stew is in bread bowls. You can often find small, crusty rounds of bread in the bakery section—if not, unsliced hoagie rolls will work. Pull the bread out of the middle, leaving a 1½-inch-thick shell. Save the bread to make crumbs. Ladle the stew right into the bread bowls. Bake apples or pears in the microwave for a warm and comforting dessert.

1 pound stew beef

1 (14-ounce) package frozen mixed onions and peppers

2 (15-ounce) cans whole potatoes, drained

1 (15-ounce) can sliced carrots, drained

1 (15-ounce) can green beans, drained

1½ cups beef broth

1 tablespoon brown sugar

2 teaspoons Worcestershire sauce

2 teaspoons tomato paste

1 teaspoon bottled minced garlic

1 teaspoon salt

¼ teaspoon freshly ground black pepper

1. To the slow cooker, dump in the stew beef, onions and peppers, potatoes, carrots, green beans, beef broth, brown sugar, Worcestershire sauce, tomato paste, garlic, salt, and pepper.

2. Cook on low for 8 hours.

TO FREEZE

1. To a large, labeled freezer-safe bag, dump in the stew beef, onions and peppers, potatoes, carrots, green beans, beef broth, brown sugar, Worcestershire sauce, tomato paste, garlic, salt, and pepper.

2. Seal the bag, flatten, and freeze flat.

3. The night before cooking, transfer the meal from the freezer to the refrigerator to thaw overnight.

4. The next morning, dump the contents of the bag into the slow cooker.

5. Cook on low for 8 hours.

> **TIP:** If you like a thicker sauce for your stew, use brown gravy instead of beef broth. If you'd like to use this recipe to make soup, use all diced vegetables, add 1 (15-ounce) can of drained peas, and add more beef broth to thin to the consistency you like. Canned, sliced mushrooms work really well in this dish if your family likes them.

ITALIAN BEEF SANDWICHES

Serves: 6 Prep time: 5 minutes Cook time: 8 to 10 hours

This may be the easiest recipe ever created. The lean beef marinates in the pepperoncini peppers and turns butter-tender by the long, slow cooking process. It also absorbs all the flavor from the peppers during that time. Serve with onion rings or chips and some sliced tomatoes. Need a dessert? Make a quick cheesecake with a purchased graham cracker crust. Mix together 8 ounces of cream cheese, 1 cup of milk, and 1 (4-serving) package of instant lemon pudding until smooth. Pour into the crust, refrigerate, and it will be ready to eat in 30 minutes.

1 (1½-pound) boneless beef eye of round

1 (12-ounce) jar sliced pepperoncini, undrained

1 cup diced onion

6 slices provolone cheese

6 hoagie rolls

1. In a slow cooker, combine the beef, pepperoncini and its brine, and onion.

2. Cook on low for 8 to 10 hours.

3. Using two forks, shred the beef in the cooker.

4. Equally divide the beef among the hoagie rolls. Top each with 1 slice of provolone cheese. Let sit for about 1 minute so the juices soak into the roll and the cheese melts.

1. To a large, labeled freezer-safe bag, add the beef, pepperoncini and its brine, and onions.

2. Seal the bag, flatten, and freeze flat.

3. The night before cooking, transfer the meal from the freezer to the refrigerator to thaw overnight.

4. The next morning, dump the contents of the bag into the slow cooker.

5. Cook on low for 8 to 10 hours.

6. Using two forks, shred the beef in the cooker.

7. Equally divide the beef among the hoagie rolls. Top each with 1 slice of provolone cheese. Let sit for about 1 minute so the juices soak into the roll and the cheese melts.

TIP: You can double this recipe and freeze half of the cooked beef for another time. Or, if you have family members with different schedules, freeze the cooked beef in ½-cup portions. Add 1 hoagie roll and the ½-cup portion to a gallon-size freezer-safe bag and freeze. You'll have individual meals whenever someone needs one!

SLOW-COOKER PEPPER STEAK

Serves: 4 to 6 Prep time: 5 minutes Cook time: 8 hours

Pepper steak is a great way to take an inexpensive cut of meat and turn it into a fork-tender meal. You can usually find beef strips marked as "beef stir-fry" in your grocery store. Serve over rice to sop up the delicious sauce. If you want to finish with something sweet, set out marshmallows, mandarin oranges, strawberries, and bananas to dip in a hot fudge sauce.

1½ pounds beef sirloin strips

1 cup beef broth

1 (14-ounce) package frozen mixed onions and peppers

1 (14.5-ounce) can stewed tomatoes, undrained

3 tablespoons soy sauce

1 tablespoon bottled minced garlic

1 teaspoon sugar

1. To a slow cooker, dump in the beef, beef broth, onions and peppers, tomatoes and their liquid, soy sauce, garlic, and sugar.

2. Cook on low for 8 hours.

TO FREEZE

1. To a large, labeled freezer-safe bag, dump in the beef, beef broth, onions and peppers, tomatoes and their liquid, soy sauce, garlic, and sugar.

2. Seal the bag, flatten, and freeze flat.

3. The night before cooking, transfer the meal from the freezer to the refrigerator to thaw overnight.

4. The next morning, dump the content of the bag into the slow cooker.

5. Cook on low for 8 hours.

TIP: If you'd like a little kick, substitute diced tomatoes with green chiles for the stewed tomatoes. Leftovers, if there are any, make an excellent soup. Just add another can of tomatoes.

DR. PEPPER PULLED PORK

Serves: 4 to 6 Prep time: 5 minutes Cook time: 8 hours

Pork tenderloin is slow cooked in a spicy sauce flavored with Dr. Pepper until it is falling apart. Use the shredded pork as a sandwich filling or serve over rice or noodles. Traditionally, pulled pork is served on sandwich buns topped with a scoop of coleslaw. This is a potato-chips-and-paper-plate kind of meal—vanilla ice cream is a great finish.

1 pound pork tenderloin

1 (12-ounce) can Dr. Pepper

½ cup barbecue sauce

1 teaspoon salt

1 teaspoon freshly ground black pepper

½ teaspoon chipotle powder

Buns, for serving

1. To a slow cooker, add the pork, Dr. Pepper, barbecue sauce, salt, pepper, and chipotle powder.

2. Cook on low for 7 hours.

3. Using two forks, shred the meat in the cooker.

4. Re-cover and cook for 1 hour more.

5. Serve in buns.

1. To a large, labeled freezer-safe bag, add the pork, barbecue sauce, salt, pepper, and chipotle powder.

2. Seal the bag, flatten, and freeze flat.

3. The night before cooking, transfer the meal from the freezer to the refrigerator to thaw overnight.

4. The next morning, dump the contents of the bag into the slow cooker.

5. Add the Dr. Pepper.

6. Cook on low for 7 hours.

7. Using two forks, shred the meat in the cooker.

8. Re-cover and cook for 1 hour more.

9. Serve in buns.

> **TIP:** If you're not a fan of Dr. Pepper, ginger ale, cola, or root beer are all good substitutes. Each gives the meat a slightly different flavor, so experiment to see which you like best.

SMOTHERED PORK CHOPS

Serves: 4 to 6 Prep time: 5 minutes Cook time: 8 hours

Tender, boneless pork chops cooked in a rich mushroom gravy make a comforting meal that tastes like it took hours to make. Technically, it does, but the slow cooker does all the work. Mashed potatoes are fantastic on the side, and they don't have to take forever, either. Make instant mashed potatoes with half cream and half chicken broth in place of the water called for in the package directions. Use plenty of butter for a creamy, homemade flavor.

....

4 (4- to 6-ounce) boneless pork loin chops

1 cup diced onion

1 (10.5-ounce) can condensed cream of mushroom soup

1 (4.5-ounce) can sliced mushrooms, drained

½ cup beef broth

½ teaspoon smoked paprika

....

1. To a slow cooker, add the pork loin chops, onion, cream of mushroom soup, mushrooms, beef broth, and paprika.

2. Cook on low for 8 hours.

TO FREEZE

1. To a large, labeled freezer-safe bag, add the pork loin chops, onion, cream of mushroom soup, mushrooms, and paprika.

Seal the bag, flatten, and freeze flat.

2.

3. The night before cooking, transfer the meal from the freezer to the refrigerator to thaw overnight.

4. The next morning, dump the contents of the bag into the slow cooker.

5. Add the beef broth.

6. Cook on low for 8 hours.

TIP: Pork roast, chicken breast, or even chuck roast can be substituted for the pork chops in this recipe.

7 *Dump It in a Bowl*

· · · · · · · · · · · · ·

THERE ARE TIMES when the idea of a hot meal is as
unappealing as the thought of cooking it—sticky August
days come to mind. Salads are lifesavers when it is 95
degrees and the humidity is so high you can drink the
air with a straw. There's no need to cook anything, no
need to heat up the kitchen, and no need to exert
yourself enough to break a sweat.

Using prewashed bags of salad available in your
grocery store is not only quick and easy, but also a
good way to introduce a variety of greens—from leaf
lettuces with baby herbs to classic romaine lettuce—
into your mealtimes. Any salad green called for in the
following recipes can be substituted with any other
type.

If you're making salads for lunches or picnics, layer
them in a 1-quart canning jar. Salad dressing goes in
first, then the heaviest ingredients on the bottom, and
layer the lightest ingredients on up. These keep in the
refrigerator up to one week, unless you have foods like

avocado in them—then you'll need to eat the salad within a day or so.

GREEK CHICKEN SALAD

Serves: 4 Prep time: 5 minutes

Greek food is full of bright, Mediterranean flavor, and this salad is no different. Salty Kalamata olives, sweet tomatoes, and spicy chicken are combined with other ingredients and coated in a tangy Greek dressing. Pick up a baguette and some garlic butter at the store to serve alongside. Chilled melon slices are a sweet finish to this meal.

1 pound cooked chicken fajita strips

16 ounces romaine lettuce salad

1½ cups cherry tomatoes

1½ cups diced cucumber

1 red onion, sliced

¾ cup Kalamata olives, pitted and drained

¾ cup pepperoncini peppers, drained

4 ounces feta cheese

1½ cups Greek salad dressing

1. In a bowl, dump and toss the chicken, romaine lettuce, cherry tomatoes, cucumber, red onion, olives, pepperoncini, feta cheese, and salad dressing until everything is evenly coated with the dressing.

2. Serve.

TIP: You can substitute peeled, deveined, and cooked shrimp for the chicken. Baby spinach leaves are a great substitute for the romaine lettuce and significantly increase the nutrition in this dish. Several brands of Greek salad dressings are available at most grocery stores, but you can also use a zesty Italian if you prefer.

CHICKEN AND STRAWBERRY SALAD

Serves: 4 Prep time: 5 minutes

This is tearoom food—perfect for an afternoon tea, lunch with friends, or a quick and easy dinner. The flavors are perfectly balanced—from the sweetness of a perfectly ripe strawberry to the brininess of the cheese. Serve tearoom-style with an oversized bakery lemon muffin on the side. Since this is such a simple salad, use only the ripest and freshest ingredients you can.

1 (12-ounce) bag mixed salad greens

2 cups chopped cooked chicken

1 (15-ounce) can mandarin oranges, drained

8 ounces fresh strawberries, washed, hulled, and quartered

1 cup pecan halves

2 ounces crumbled blue cheese, feta cheese, or goat cheese

1 cup poppy seed dressing

1. In a large bowl, gently combine the salad greens, chicken, oranges, strawberries, pecans, blue cheese, and poppy seed dressing until everything is evenly coated with the dressing.

2. Serve.

TIP: Give this a tropical twist by substituting drained pineapple chunks for the strawberries and using macadamia nuts in place of the pecans. Cooked shrimp can be substituted for the chicken, if you prefer. Serve your tropical-inspired salad with a banana muffin on the side.

BARBECUE CHICKEN SALAD

Serves: 4 Prep time: 5 minutes

Red-checkered tablecloths, picnic tables, and ice-cold beer come to mind when you first taste this all-American dish. If you have a minute or two to spare, add a charred flavor to the corn by placing it in a single layer on a baking sheet and running a kitchen torch over the corn until it begins to blacken in a few places. Serve with cornbread and warm peach pie filling over vanilla ice cream for a good old-fashioned country flavor.

½ cup ranch dressing

½ cup barbecue sauce

2 cups cooked rotisserie barbecued chicken

1 (12-ounce) bag romaine lettuce salad

1 (15-ounce) can black beans, drained and rinsed

1 cup canned corn

1 cup red onion, sliced into rings

1 cup shredded Monterey Jack cheese

2 cups corn chips

1. In a small bowl, mix together the ranch dressing and the barbecue sauce. Set aside.

2. In a large bowl, combine the chicken, romaine lettuce, black beans, corn, red onion, and Monterey Jack cheese.

3. Pour the dressing over the salad. Toss lightly until all the ingredients are evenly coated with the dressing.

4. Gently stir in the corn chips and serve.

TIP: Ranch-style beans can be substituted for the black beans. They have lots of smoky flavor that brings out the barbecue characteristics of this dish. Drain them but don't rinse them—the sauce contributes to the flavor.

FAJITA SALAD BOWLS

Serves: 4 Prep time: 5 minutes Cook time: 5 minutes

These easy rice bowls can be served immediately or frozen in microwave-safe containers to be eaten at a later date. If you do freeze them, omit the sour cream and avocado until ready to serve. A bowl of tortilla chips, salsa, and guacamole make the perfect sides to this meal. Cool off with mango sherbet or sorbet.

1 (16-ounce) package frozen chimichurri rice

1 (12-ounce) package frozen fajita onions and peppers, thawed

1 (15-ounce) can black beans, drained and rinsed, divided

1 (4-ounce) can sliced jalapeños, divided

2 cups cooked chicken fajita strips, divided

1 cup sour cream, divided

1 cup diced avocado, divided

1 cup shredded Mexican-blend cheese, divided

Lime slices, for garnishing

1. Heat the chimichurri rice according to the package directions. Divide the hot rice among 4 bowls.

2. To each bowl, add ¼ of the onions and peppers, ¼ of the black beans, ¼ of the jalapenos, and ¼ cup of chicken.

3. Garnish each serving with ¼ cup of sour cream, ¼ cup of avocado, and ¼ cup of Mexican-blend cheese.

4. Serve with lime slices to squeeze over the top.

TIP: Cooked beef fajita strips can be used instead of the chicken. If you can't find chimichurri rice in the freezer section, use cilantro-lime rice or plain rice instead.

ASIAN CHICKEN SALAD

Serves: 4 to 6 Prep time: 5 minutes

Asian chicken salad is a quick, easy summer meal. Pick up some egg rolls at the deli and you are good to go. Serve a simple dessert of fresh fruit, such as red seedless grapes or melon. Of course, fortune cookies are always a fun finish to this Asian-inspired meal.

- -

2 cups cooked rotisserie lemon chicken

1 (12-ounce) package broccoli slaw

½ cup chopped smoked almonds

1 (8-ounce) can mandarin oranges, drained

1 cup sesame-ginger salad dressing

1 (6-ounce) container crunchy chow mein noodles

- -

1. In a large bowl, combine the chicken, broccoli slaw, almonds, oranges, and sesame-ginger dressing. Mix until all the ingredients are evenly coated with the dressing.

2. Gently stir in the chow mein noodles. Serve immediately.

> **TIP:** If you prefer a traditional cabbage slaw to the broccoli slaw, it's fine to substitute one for the other. The almonds lend a salty, smoky flavor to this dish, but if that's not your preference, substitute regular almonds, pecans, or any other nut you like. Once the chow mein noodles are incorporated, the salad needs to be eaten soon or they

get soggy. Don't keep any leftovers if they include the chow mein noodles.

BURRITO BOWLS

Serves: 4 Prep time: 5 minutes Cook time: 5 minutes

All of the delicious flavor of a burrito is incorporated into a bowl. This yummy Tex-Mex-inspired dish is sure to become a regular part of your meal plan. Serve with a stack of warm flour tortillas and plenty of butter or tortilla chips and salsa. For an authentic dessert, look for churros in the freezer section of your grocery store. Serve the churros with hot fudge sauce to dip them in.

- 1 (16-ounce) package frozen rice, heated according to package directions
- 1 cup chunky salsa
- 1 (12-ounce) package salad mix, divided
- 1 (15.25-ounce) can corn, drained, divided
- 1 (15-ounce) can pinto beans, drained and rinsed, divided
- 2 cups cooked ground beef, divided
- 1 cup cherry tomatoes, divided
- 1 cup shredded Mexican-blend cheese, divided
- 1 cup sour cream, divided
- 1 cup diced avocado, divided
- ¼ cup fresh cilantro leaves, divided

1. In a medium bowl, stir together the rice and salsa. Divide the mixture among 4 bowls.

2. Top each with ¼ of the salad mix, ¼ of the corn, and ¼ of the

pinto beans.

3. Add ½ cup of ground beef, ¼ cup of cherry tomatoes, ¼ cup of cheese, ¼ cup of sour cream, and ¼ cup of avocado to each bowl.

4. Garnish each with 1 tablespoon of cilantro.

5. Serve immediately.

TIP: These flavorful bowls can easily be made vegetarian by omitting the ground beef and doubling the amount of pinto beans. You can also substitute cooked chicken or fajita beef for the ground beef in this recipe.

CALYPSO BEEF SALAD

Serves: 4 Prep time: 5 minutes

This salad is a taste of the tropics with pineapple, orange, lime, and a touch of spicy Jamaican jerk seasoning. Of course, adjust the amount of seasoning to satisfy your heat tolerance. Serve with sweet Hawaiian rolls and a bakery coconut cream pie to cool things down. Whole-grain crackers, a soft Brie cheese, and fresh fruit round out this meal. Cue the steel drums.

....

1 (12-ounce) bag mixed baby greens salad

1 pound cooked beef fajita strips

1 (8-ounce) can pineapple chunks, drained

1 (8-ounce) can mandarin oranges, drained

3 tablespoons freshly squeezed lime juice

½ cup peach-mango salsa

½ cup corn

½ cup diced onion

½ cup diced green bell pepper

¼ cup chopped fresh cilantro

1 teaspoon Jamaican jerk seasoning

Red grapes on the vine, for garnishing, divided

....

1. Evenly divide the salad greens among 4 plates.

2. In a large bowl, gently combine the beef, pineapple, oranges, lime juice, peach-mango salsa, corn, onion, bell pepper, cilantro,

and jerk seasoning.

3. Spoon equal amounts over each salad plate.

4. Garnish each with a small cluster of grapes. Serve immediately.

> **TIP:** Peeled and deveined cooked shrimp can be substituted for the beef. If using shrimp, toss it in the salsa and allow it to marinate for 15 minutes. The finished dish will have a lot more flavor.

WHITE BEAN AND TUNA SALAD PROVENÇAL

Serves: 4 Prep time: 5 minutes

A traditional French salad with an untraditional twist, this tuna salad is fresh and bright with the flavors of the Mediterranean. You can buy shelled hard-boiled eggs at many grocery delis, which makes this dish almost effortless. Serve with a crusty baguette, garlic butter, and a good red wine for a romantic and relaxing summer meal. Fruit tarts from the local bakery add that touch of something sweet for the perfect ending to your meal.

1 (12-ounce) package baby salad greens with herbs

2 hard-boiled eggs, quartered

1 (14.5-ounce) can white beans, drained and rinsed

2 (5-ounce) cans albacore tuna

1 cup cherry tomatoes

½ cup chopped red onion

½ cup Kalamata olives

1 teaspoon dried Herbes de Provence

½ cup red wine vinaigrette

1. Evenly divide the salad greens among 4 plates.

2. Add 2 egg pieces to each plate.

3. In a large bowl, gently combine the white beans, tuna, cherry tomatoes, red onion, olives, Herbes de Provence, and red wine

vinaigrette.

4. Place one-quarter of the tuna mixture on each plate. Serve immediately.

TIP: Cooked chicken breast, scallops, or shrimp can be substituted for the tuna. This salad also makes a fantastic sandwich. Cut a sourdough baguette lengthwise, scoop out some of the insides, spoon in the tuna mixture, add sliced eggs on top, and a bit of the salad. Top with the other loaf half, slice, and enjoy.

SOUTHWESTERN BLACK BEAN SALAD
VEGETARIAN

Serves: 4 to 6 **Prep time:** *5 minutes*

When you want something filling, but also light and healthy, this is your go-to salad. Beans and corn combine to create a complete protein, while tomatoes, chiles, and onion give it bright flavor. Serve with tortilla chips, warm flour tortillas, or even garlic bread. If you want a quick dessert, sandwich two pecan shortbread cookies together with chocolate-hazelnut spread.

1 (15-ounce) can black beans, drained and rinsed

1 (15-ounce) can kidney beans, drained and rinsed

1 (10.5-ounce) can diced tomatoes with green chiles

1 cup fresh, frozen, or canned corn

1 diced avocado

½ cup chopped red onion

½ cup chopped fresh cilantro

1 cup Catalina salad dressing

Chopped lettuce, for serving (optional)

1. In a large bowl, gently combine the black beans, kidney beans, tomatoes with green chiles, corn, avocado, onion, cilantro, and Catalina dressing.

2. Serve as-is or over chopped lettuce (if using).

TIP: If you want a slightly heartier non-vegetarian salad, this is delicious with grilled chicken breast or cooked shrimp. It also makes a great filling for tortilla or lettuce wraps. Add some jalapeños if you want to spice it up. It's even better the next day!

SEVEN-LAYER SALAD

Serves: 6 Prep time: 10 minutes Chill time: 8 hours

This salad goes together fast, but it does have to be refrigerated overnight, which makes it a good make-ahead meal. This dish goes fast at potlucks! Serve with onion rolls for a complete meal. All you really need to finish is some ice-cold watermelon.

. . . .

1 (12-ounce) bag classic salad mix

3 hard-boiled eggs, sliced

1 cup frozen peas, thawed

1 red onion, chopped

½ cup chopped celery

½ cup chopped green pepper

1¼ cups coleslaw dressing

4 slices cooked bacon, crumbled

1½ cups shredded Cheddar cheese

. . . .

1. In a large glass bowl, dump the salad mix in the bottom.

2. Cover with the egg slices.

3. Spoon the peas over the eggs.

4. Cover the peas with the red onion.

5. Top with the celery.

6. Spread the green pepper over the celery.

7. Cover with the coleslaw dressing.

8. Sprinkle with the bacon.

9. Finish by topping with the Cheddar cheese.

10. Cover with plastic wrap and refrigerate for 8 hours, or overnight.

Measurement Conversions

Volume Equivalents (Liquid)

US STANDARD	US STANDARD (OUNCES)	METRIC (APPROXIMATE)
2 tablespoons	1 fl. oz.	30 mL
¼ cup	2 fl. oz.	60 mL
½ cup	4 fl. oz.	120 mL
1 cup	8 fl. oz.	240 mL
1½ cups	12 fl. oz.	355 mL
2 cups or 1 pint	16 fl. oz.	475 mL
4 cups or 1 quart	32 fl. oz.	1 L
1 gallon	128 fl. oz.	4 L

Volume Equivalents (Dry)

US STANDARD	METRIC (APPROXIMATE)
⅛ teaspoon	0.5 mL
¼ teaspoon	1 mL
½ teaspoon	2 mL
¾ teaspoon	4 mL
1 teaspoon	5 mL
1 tablespoon	15 mL
¼ cup	59 mL
⅓ cup	79 mL
½ cup	118 mL
⅔ cup	156 mL
¾ cup	177 mL
1 cup	235 mL
2 cups or 1 pint	475 mL
3 cups	700 mL
4 cups or 1 quart	1 L
½ gallon	2 L
1 gallon	4 L

Oven Temperatures

FAHRENHEIT (F)	CELSIUS (C) (APPROXIMATE)
250°	120°
300°	150°
325°	165°
350°	180°
375°	190°
400°	200°
425°	220°
450°	230°

Weight Equivalents

US STANDARD	METRIC (APPROXIMATE)
½ ounce	15 g
1 ounce	30 g
2 ounces	60 g
4 ounces	115 g
8 ounces	225 g
12 ounces	340 g
16 ounces or 1 pound	455 g

Printed in Dunstable, United Kingdom

76513464R00125